Family Favourites

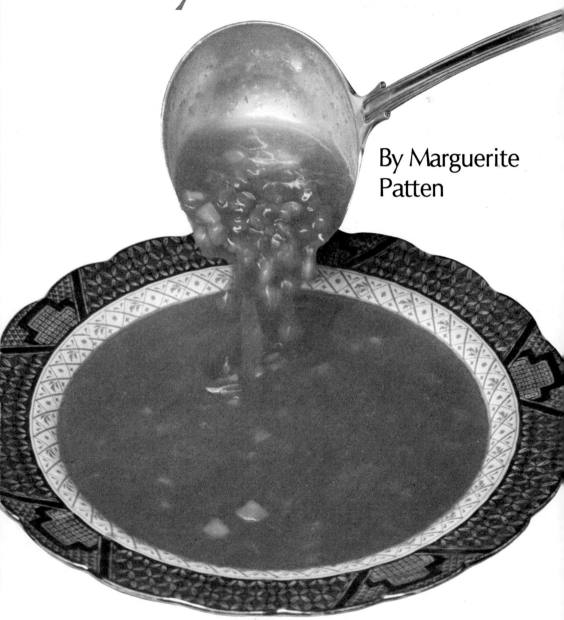

By Marguerite Patten

Octopus Books

Contents

Title page: CHICKEN NOODLE SOUP

First published 1973 by Octopus Books Limited
59 Grosvenor Street, London W 1

ISBN 0 7064 0226 X

© 1973 Octopus Books Limited

Some recipes and illustrations in this book were originally published
in 'Perfect Cooking' by Marguerite Patten

Produced by Mandarin Publishers Ltd
77a Marble Road, North Point, Hong Kong
and printed in Hong Kong

WEIGHTS
AND MEASURES

All measurements in this book are based on Imperial weights and measures.

When a cup measurement is used, this refers to a cup of 8 fl. oz. capacity.

1 Imperial pint = 20 fl. oz.

Level spoon measurements are used in all the recipes.

Metric measures: for easy reference

1 kilogramme (1000 grammes) = 2.2 lb

$\frac{1}{2}$ kilogramme (500 grammes) = 1 lb (working equivalent)

1 litre = $1\frac{3}{4}$ pints (working equivalent)

$\frac{1}{2}$ litre = 1 pint (working equivalent)

Acknowledgments

Photographs on pages 27, 31, 33, 92, 96, 97, 101, 117 by John Lee.

Photographs on pages 1, 5, 19, 23, 41, 45, 51, 55, 65, 73, 80, 88, 89, 104, 113, 124, 125 by Syndication International.

Introduction

You will probably find that over the years members of the family have developed a liking for certain foods or dishes and they become firm favourites, to be served on many occasions.

Because of these definite likes and dislikes there may be a tendency for family menus to become slightly monotonous, but with a little ingenuity you will be able to adapt those 'all too well known recipes', so they become something new, without losing their appeal. This book concentrates on practical and imaginative dishes for the family, as well as giving hints on cooking some of the most important foods.

You will find hints on some of the pages, for ways in which you can save money in cooking the particular dishes in that section, also short cuts for the busy home-maker, and ways to adapt certain dishes for the younger members of the family.

Each age group in a family has specific needs from the food they eat. Young children and the very old must have adequate nourishment in an easily digested form; that is why milk is so important in their diets. Growing children and young adults need plenty of protein, fruit, green vegetables, but require a sensible amount of bread and other carbo-hydrate foods to satisfy their healthy appetites. All too often the middle-aged must cut down on calories (fats and carbohydrate foods in particular) to counteract a tendency to become over-weight.

Proteins are essential for us all since they ensure healthy growth in a child and maintain health in an adult. Meats, including poultry and game, fish, cheese and eggs are the most usual sources, but certain vegetables such as peas, beans and lentils, contain a generous amount of protein and so does milk.

Correctly cooked or raw green vegetables, raw fruit, etc. are essential, for these give Vitamin C which builds up resistance to illness. Encourage children to eat these foods. They may not like cooked vegetables, but will eat them raw in an interesting salad. If a child does not like orange juice, why not make your own fresh fruit iced lollies? Unless members of your family are over-weight, give reasonable amounts of carbohydrates, in particular bread, which is a good source of the Vitamin B group, aids digestion and the nervous system, and potatoes, which give Vitamin C. Make sure the family has an adequate amount of fat such as butter and margarine, which helps to create warmth in the body.

CAULIFLOWER WITH BROWN SAUCE TOPPING

Family Soups

Make sure that family soups are sustaining and nutritious. Use seasonal vegetables and stock made from simmering bones or carcasses of chicken – this saves buying stock cubes. Add milk to the soup where suitable – this is an excellent way to disguise milk for members of the family who do not drink this.

Onion and Pepper Soup

2 large onions
1–2 cloves garlic (optional)
2 tablespoons oil, or 2 oz.
  ($\frac{1}{4}$ cup) butter or margarine
1 large green and 1 large red
  pepper
1$\frac{1}{2}$ pints (4 cups) brown or white
  stock or water

2 large tomatoes
2–4 oz. ($\frac{1}{2}$–1 cup mushrooms
seasoning
Garnish:
chopped herbs
grated cheese or croûtons,
  see page 7

Peel the onions and cut into narrow strips. Peel and crush the garlic cloves. Heat the oil or butter or margarine and toss the onion and garlic in this until nearly transparent. Take care the onions do not brown.

Discard the cores and seeds from the peppers and cut the pulp, or flesh, into small strips. Blend with the onion but do not fry if you like a firm texture.

Add the liquid, bring steadily to the boil. Add the skinned chopped tomatoes and sliced mushrooms. Continue cooking until the vegetables are soft. Season well.

Serve while very hot. Garnish with chopped fresh herbs, grated cheese or croûtons.

Serves 4–6.

Variations:
Use all onions and brown stock.
Use all mushrooms and brown stock.

6

Chicken Noodle Soup

carcass of a chicken
about 2½–3 pints (6⅔–8 cups)
  water to cover
seasoning
1–2 onions
1–2 carrots

bouquet garni
3–4 tablespoons shell noodles
1 oz. (¼ cup) flour
Garnish:
fried croûtons, see below

Put the chicken carcass, plus the giblets, less the liver, if available, into a saucepan. Cover with water, add seasoning, prepared vegetables and herbs. Bring the liquid to the boil, cover the pan and simmer for at least 2 hours or, if using a pressure cooker, allow about 40 minutes at 15 lb. pressure. Strain the stock. Any small pieces of chicken can be chopped or sieved and added to the stock just before serving. Add the noodles and cook steadily for 15 minutes or until tender. Blend the flour with a little stock, put into the pan with the remainder of the stock and cook until slightly thickened, stirring well. Serve hot topped with croûtons.
Serves 5–6.

To make croûtons:
Either dice toasted bread or dice bread and fry in hot oil or cooking fat until crisp and golden brown. Drain on absorbent paper.

To make garlic croûtons:
Fry as above, then roll in garlic salt.

Variations:
Chicken Soup: Ingredients as above but omit the noodles.
Cream of Chicken Soup: Ingredients as above but omit the noodles and use 1½ pints (4 cups) water only. Simmer the giblets, etc. as above. Strain and sieve any tiny pieces of chicken and add to the liquid. Blend the flour in the recipe with ½ pint (1⅓ cups) milk. Stir into the chicken liquid with 1–2 oz. butter or margarine and cook until thickened. Taste, add more seasoning if required. Add a little cream before serving.

Chinese-Style Vegetable Soup

1 tablespoon corn oil or olive oil
3 tablespoons long grain rice
2 pints (5⅓ cups) chicken stock,
   or water and 2–3 chicken stock
   cubes

seasoning
1 small carrot
1 small turnip
small piece swede
1–2 sticks celery
Garnish:
chopped parsley

Heat the oil in a saucepan. Add the rice and turn in the oil for several minutes. Pour the stock into the pan, or the water and stock cubes, bring to the boil. Stir briskly, add seasoning. Lower the heat and cover the pan. Simmer gently for 20 minutes, until the rice is just tender.
Grate the vegetables finely or coarsely according to personal taste, add to the soup and heat for a few minutes only so the vegetables retain their firm texture. Add extra seasoning if required. Serve topped with parsley.
Serves 4–6.

Variation:
Add yogurt to the soup just before serving.

Rice and Lemon Soup

2 pints (5⅓ cups) chicken stock
3 tablespoons long grain rice
1 or 2 lemons

seasoning
Garnish:
chopped parsley

Simmer the stock with the rice, lemon juice and ½–1 teaspoon finely grated lemon rind for 20–25 minutes. Season well and top with parsley.
Serves 4–6.

For slimmers:
Avoid as much rice as possible.

8   CHINESE STYLE VEGETABLE SOUP *(Photograph by American Rice Council)*

Cooking Fish

Fish is an excellent protein food and has the added advantage of being easy to digest. If members of your family are not particularly fond of fish then try new ways of presenting it. The rolled fillets of fish on page 18 look much more exciting than ordinary pieces of fried fish.
Many children who normally do not eat fish will enjoy the fish cakes on page 14. These may be given additional food value by adding a small quantity of grated cheese to the fish mixture before forming into the flat cakes.

Spiced Herrings

4 large or 8 small herrings
1 onion
1 sweet dessert apple
1–2 teaspoons mixed spice

$\frac{1}{2}$ pint ($1\frac{1}{3}$ cups) apple juice or cider
Garnish:
chopped parsley
gherkins

Remove the heads and bones from the herrings, see page 12. Divide each herring into 2 fillets. Roll these up and put into a fairly deep oven-proof dish. Slice or chop the onion, core the apple and put with the herrings. Blend the spice with the apple juice or cider. Pour over the fish, cover the dish. Bake for approximately 1 hour in the centre of a very moderate oven, 325–350°F, Mark 3–4. Serve hot or cold, topped with parsley and gherkin fans.
Serves 4.

For slimmers:
Choose the spiced herrings as there is no fat in the recipe. Use vinegar in place of apple juice if wished.
Children often enjoy herrings and both these recipes should appeal. Herrings are a particularly nutritious fish.

Fish Kebabs

This method of cooking fish is ideal for firm fleshed white fish, such as cod, hake, haddock, etc. Skin the fish, cut into neat pieces. Frozen fish should be thawed out sufficiently to dice neatly. Put on to well greased metal skewers with tiny tomatoes, mushrooms, rings of green pepper or even tiny boiled potatoes. Brush with melted butter or margarine or oil flavoured with salt, pepper and a squeeze of lemon juice. Put under the grill and cook until the fish is tender. Remove from the skewers with a fork before you eat the very hot food.

Sardine Bake

Fresh sardines and fresh sprats have a very sweet flavour, which most people enjoy. Bone and take the heads off the fish, put into a greased oven-proof dish; season, then cover with sliced tomatoes plus a little grated onion and breadcrumbs. Top with melted butter and bake for about 20 minutes in a moderate oven.

Fried Herrings in Oatmeal

4 large herrings
1 oz. ($\frac{1}{4}$ cup) flour or oatmeal,
  or rolled oats
seasoning

cooking fat for frying
Garnish:
parsley
lemon

Remove the heads from the fish, clean and remove the back bone as instructions on page 12, wash and dry well. Mix the flour, oatmeal or rolled oats with seasoning and coat the herrings in this. Heat the cooking fat in a pan and fry the herrings for 3–5 minutes on either side. Drain on absorbent paper and garnish with parsley and lemon.
Serves 4.

Normandy Herrings

4 large herrings
seasoning
1 oz. ($\frac{1}{4}$ cup) flour
3 oz. ($\frac{3}{8}$ cup) butter or margarine

1 large onion
2–3 dessert apples
1 tablespoon lemon juice
Garnish:
parsley

Remove the heads from the fish, clean and remove the back
bone, if wished, see instructions below. Season the flour and
roll the fish in this.
Heat about 2 oz. ($\frac{1}{4}$ cup) of the butter or margarine in a large
pan. Peel and chop the onion. Core the apples, slice 1 apple
into rings for garnish, and chop the remainder. Fry the apples
and onions in the pan until the apples are soft and the onion
is transparent. Add the lemon juice. Put the chopped onions
and apples into a hot serving dish and keep warm; keeping
the apple slices for garnish separate. Heat the remaining
butter or margarine in the frying pan and cook the fish until
tender. Put the fish on top of the mixture in the serving dish
and garnish with the apple slices and parsley.
Serves 4.

Variation:
Use shelled prawns in place of the apples and onion. Fry the
fish first, remove and keep warm, then fry the prawns in the
cleaned pan in a little extra butter. Add 1–2 tablespoons
Chablis or Calvados and spoon over the fish.

To bone herring:
Cut the head off the fish, remove the intestines and wash well.
Save the roe to use with the fish. Wash in cold water. Split the
fish along the belly. Open out and lay on a wooden surface
with the cut side downwards, then run your fingers firmly
along the back bone. Turn the fish over and you will find you
can remove the bones very easily.

NORMANDY HERRINGS *(Photograph by Herring Industry Board)*

Fish Cakes

8 oz. cooked fish*
8 oz. (1 cup) creamed potatoes
1 egg
seasoning
Coating:
$\frac{1}{2}$ oz. flour

1 egg
approximately 2 oz. ($\frac{2}{3}$ cup)
 crisp breadcrumbs
about 2 oz. ($\frac{1}{4}$ cup) cooking fat,
 or 2 tablespoons oil for frying

*White fish, herrings, kippers, tuna (canned or fresh) or salmon (canned or fresh) may be used.

Flake the cooked fish finely, blend with the potatoes, the egg and seasoning. Form into 8 flat cakes. Coat with the flour, blended with a little seasoning, and then with the egg and breadcrumbs. Pat into a good shape with a flat-bladed knife. Heat the cooking fat or oil in a frying pan and fry the fish cakes until crisp and brown on both sides. Drain on absorbent paper and serve hot with lemon or with a sauce, see page 15. **Serves 4.**

Variations:

Bind with a thick white sauce, as the recipe for Fish in a Jacket, see below, instead of the egg.
Add 1–2 tablespoons chopped parsley to the fish mixture.
Bind the fish cakes with about 4 tablespoons fresh, well seasoned tomato purée instead of egg.
Flavoured with 2–3 teaspoons chopped chives.

Fish in a Jacket

Make a thick white sauce, see page 15, but use only $\frac{1}{4}$ pint ($\frac{2}{3}$ cup) milk to the margarine or butter and flour. Blend this with about 8–10 oz. (1–1$\frac{1}{4}$ cups) flaked cooked fish, 2 chopped hard boiled eggs and seasoning. Make short crust pastry with 10 oz. (2$\frac{1}{2}$ cups) flour, see page 85, and roll out to a large oblong shape. Lift on to a baking tray then cover half the pastry with the fish mixture. Brush the edges with water, seal and bake for 35 minutes in a moderately hot oven, 375–400°F, Mark 5–6. **Serves 4.**

Sauces to serve with Fish

Choose fairly mild flavoured sauces to serve with fish, because too definite a flavour will overwhelm the delicate taste of the fish.

White sauce:
This is given in full below. It is an excellent basis for many sauces. Make the sauce then add the flavourings required.

Tartare sauce:
This is the accepted accompaniment to fried fish. The easiest method of producing this sauce is to blend finely chopped parsley, chopped gherkins and whole or chopped capers with mayonnaise or salad dressing.

White Sauce

1 oz. margarine or butter
1 oz. ($\frac{1}{4}$ cup) flour

$\frac{1}{2}$ pint ($1\frac{1}{3}$ cups) milk
seasoning

Heat the margarine or butter in a pan. Remove from the heat, and stir in the flour. Return to heat and cook gently for several minutes, stirring well. Remove once again from the heat and blend in the milk. Return to heat and bring to the boil and cook until thickened, stirring or whisking to give a smooth sauce. Add seasoning to taste.
Serves 3–4.

Variations:
Flavour the sauce with anchovy essence, chopped parsley, grated cheese, etc. Do not boil again after adding the cheese.

For slimmers:
Use skimmed milk in the sauce, and stir a little thin cream into the thickened sauce for the rest of the family.

15

Stuffed Plaice in Cream

1 lb. (2 cups) cooked mashed
   potatoes
seasoning
2 oz. ($\frac{1}{4}$ cup) butter
4 large or 8 small plaice fillets

3 oz. ($\frac{3}{4}$ cup) mushrooms
3–4 rashers lean bacon
$\frac{1}{4}$ pint ($\frac{2}{3}$ cup) thick cream
Garnish:
tomato
parsley

Beat the potatoes with seasoning and 1 oz. butter. Put into a
cloth bag with a $\frac{1}{4}$ or $\frac{1}{2}$-inch potato rose (large nozzle), and
pipe a border round the edge of a shallow oven-proof dish.
Skin the fillets of plaice, or ask the fishmonger to do this. If
using frozen fish allow to defrost. Slice the mushrooms and
chop the bacon. Heat the remaining butter and fry the
mushrooms and bacon in this for a few minutes. Spoon into
the centre of the fish rolls. Roll up the fillets from the tail to
the head, securing with wooden cocktail sticks and put into
the dish. Season the cream. Pour over the fish. Cover the dish
lightly with foil, do not press this down and spoil the potato
piping. Bake in the centre of a moderate oven, 350–375°F,
Mark 4–5, for 15 minutes until the fish is tender; do not
over-cook.
Meanwhile halve the tomato or cut in a Van-Dyke design, and
bake for a few minutes in the oven. Remove the foil and
cocktail sticks from the fillets, and garnish with the tomato
and parsley. Serve at once.
Serves 4.

Variations:
Omit the cream in the recipe above and use a white sauce
made with 1 oz. butter or margarine, 1 oz. ($\frac{1}{4}$ cup) flour and
$\frac{1}{2}$ pint ($1\frac{1}{3}$ cups) milk, or milk and fish stock.
As a change make the sauce with $\frac{1}{2}$ pint ($1\frac{1}{3}$ cups) tomato
juice instead of milk.
Omit the mushroom and bacon stuffing and use a packet of
parsley and thyme mixture, or a little flaked canned tuna fish
or salmon.

STUFFED PLAICE IN CREAM *(Photograph by National Dairy Council)*   **17**

Rolled Fillets of Fish

8 medium fillets of skinned white
fish

coating (a) or (b), see below
cooking fat or oil, see below

Roll the fillets and secure with wooden cocktail sticks. Dip in
the selected coating (a) or (b); remove the sticks before frying.
(a) **Egg and breadcrumb coating**: Coat fish with seasoned
flour and then with beaten egg and fine crisp breadcrumbs.
You can use fine soft crumbs if preferred. It is a good idea to
coat the fish with a very thin layer of flour before the egg, as
this helps the final coating to adhere to the fish. 1 egg plus
about 2 oz. ($\frac{1}{2}$ cup) crisp breadcrumbs should coat 4 portions
(8 small to medium fillets).
(b) **Batter coating**: The following quantities are enough to
coat 4 portions (8 small to medium fillets). Sieve 4 oz. (1 cup)
flour, plain or self-raising, with a pinch salt. Add 1 egg and
about 12 tablespoons milk, or milk and water. When coating
in batter, dip the fish in seasoned flour first. Dip in the batter;
allow any surplus batter to drop back into the basin.
Serves 4 as a main dish.

Cooking fat or oil for frying:
Make sure the pan of cooking fat or oil is not over-filled, as
the level will rise when the fish is placed into the pan. Test
the temperature of the cooking fat or oil, it should be 365°F.
Place the empty frying basket into the hot cooking fat or oil so
it becomes coated, as this prevents the fish sticking to the
mesh. Lift the warmed basket from the cooking fat or oil, and
lower the coated fish into this.

Timing:
Thick or rolled fillets take about 4 minutes. Thin fillets take
about 3 minutes. Thick steaks or whole fish take about 5–6
minutes.
Lift the fish from the pan and allow the basket to remain over
the top of the pan for a few seconds for any surplus fat to drop
back into the pan. Drain on absorbent paper and serve. Deep
fried fish can be served with tartare sauce, see page 15.

18

Seafood Pie

1½ lb. white fish, inexpensive kind
about ½ pint (1⅓ cups) fish stock or water
seasoning
Sauce:
2 oz. (¼ cup) margarine or butter

2 oz. (½ cup) flour
1 pint (2⅔ cups) milk, or milk and fish stock
few prawns
about 1 lb. (2 cups) creamed potato
little butter or margarine

Poach the fish, either in the fish stock or in the water and seasoning. Drain and flake the fish; use the liquid as part of the sauce if wished. Make the sauce as the recipe on page 15. Mix the sauce and fish, add the prawns. Put into a pie dish and top with the creamed potato and a little butter or margarine. Bake for approximately 30 minutes just above the centre of a moderate to moderately hot oven, 375–400°F, Mark 5–6.
Serves 4–5.

Fish Pie Americaine

2–3 rashers streaky bacon
1–2 onions
3 tomatoes
1 oz. (¼ cup) flour

¾ pint (2 cups) chicken or fish stock
1–1½ lb. white fish
seasoning
1 lb. (2 cups) mashed potato

Chop the bacon, onions and skinned tomatoes. Fry the bacon 2–3 minutes to extract the fat. Add the onions and then the tomatoes and cook for several minutes. Stir in the flour, then gradually blend in the stock. Bring to the boil and cook until thickened. Cook the fish – either by baking or poaching in well seasoned water. Flake and add to the sauce; season well. Put into a pie dish, top with mashed potato and bake for approximately 30 minutes just above the centre of a moderate to moderately hot oven, 375–400°F, mark 5–6.
Serves 5–6.

Cooking Meat and Poultry

TO ROAST MEAT

Buy meat to give a minimum of 8–12 oz. per person, including the weight of the bone. Allow frozen meat to defrost. Wash and dry the meat. Make any stuffing required, see recipes, pages 26–28. Put the meat into a roasting tin, in foil, or on a spit. Spread any cooking fat recommended over the top of the meat. The amount of cooking fat suggested for the meats must be increased by about 2 oz. ($\frac{1}{4}$ cup) if roasting potatoes round the joint.

In an open roasting tin:
Allow the times given for each meat. You can baste with a little cooking fat during cooking, if wished. This means spooning some of the hot cooking fat over the meat. The advantage of this is that it keeps the meat moist and encourages it to crisp, but it is not essential.

In foil:
You wrap the meat and any cooking fat in the foil, and cook to the time given for the chosen meat, see pages 22–25. But you must allow about 20 minutes extra cooking time or set the oven 25°F higher, or 1 Mark higher on a gas cooker. If you wish the meat to crisp and brown, open the foil for the last 20–30 minutes. There is no need to baste during cooking.

21

In a covered roasting tin:
Try and use one large enough to give some space above and around the meat. This means the cooking fat splashes the lid, drops back on to the meat and so is self-basting; it will brown well. If required to be crisp, the lid should be removed for the last 20–30 minutes. Allow a higher temperature or extra cooking time as for foil.

Spit roasting:
Time as for slow or fast roasting, but melt the cooking fat and brush over the whole joint. Baste if wished during cooking.

Cuts of Meat and Roasting Times

The times given below assume the meat is put into a hot oven, 425–450°F, Mark 6–7, and left at that temperature for the first 20 minutes to seal the outside of the meat. After this time the oven can be reduced to moderately hot, 375–400°F, Mark 5–6.

Beef:
Choose the prime cuts, i.e. sirloin, rib, Chateaubriand (this is a luxury joint for it is a large piece of fillet steak); good quality topside. I prefer to roast sirloin and rib with no additional fat, but add about 2 oz. ($\frac{1}{4}$ cup) for Chateaubriand or topside or when I am roasting potatoes round the joint. If you like beef under-done then allow just 15 minutes per lb. and 15 minutes over in an open tin; but increase this by 5 minutes per lb. and 5 minutes over for well cooked beef. If the joint is exceptionally small (about 2 lb.) then be a little generous with your timings.
Serve beef with a thin gravy or just the meat juices, with Yorkshire pudding and horseradish sauce and/or mustard.

Lamb:
Choose leg, shoulder, loin, saddle (double loin), best end of neck and breast (this is better boned and rolled round a

stuffing). No fat is required with lamb.

Allow 20 minutes per lb. and 20 minutes over; unless you like the French tradition of having lamb slightly under-done.

A delicious way of cooking young lamb is as follows:

Roast the lamb for about 20 minutes to extract the surplus fat, pour this away. Arrange layers of thickly sliced potatoes and thinly sliced onions in the meat dish. Season each layer well, and flavour with chopped garlic or chopped parsley. Put the joint on top and continue cooking.

A simple way to give additional flavour to lamb is to sprinkle it with dried rosemary, or put sprigs of rosemary over the joint, or to insert pieces of garlic.

Mutton:

Choose the same joints as suggested for lamb, but since this meat is less tender increase the cooking time slightly or use the slower method of cooking, see page 25. Serve mutton with red currant jelly or an onion sauce (made by adding a smooth purée of onions or chopped cooked onions to a white sauce). A little onion stock may be used in the sauce instead of all milk. A rather thick gravy blends well with mutton.

Pork:

Choose leg, fillet (this is the top of the leg), bladebone (shoulder butt), spare-rib, loin.

Although fat is unnecessary for cooking pork I like to score the fat and brush this with oil or a little melted cooking fat to encourage a truly crisp crackling. A light sprinkling of salt is liked by some people.

Pork should never be undercooked, so allow 25 minutes per lb. and 25 minutes over.

Serve pork with apple or other fruit sauce, sage and onion stuffing and a thickened gravy.

Stoned, cooked prunes blend well with pork. Add to the baking tin towards the end of the cooking time, pouring away any surplus fat first.

Instead of prunes, roast halved oranges, or dessert apples halved or whole, cored but not peeled. These may be filled with dried fruit, or just sprinkled lightly with chopped fresh sage.

Veal:
Choose leg, fillet (thick slice from the top of the leg), loin, best end of neck, breast.
Veal is exceptionally lean so must have plenty of fat. You can cover the joint with fat bacon or use butter or other cooking fat, or follow the French method of putting thin strips of fat pork through a 'larding' needle and pulling these through the meat; in this way you have an even distribution of fat basting the meat during cooking.
Allow 25 minutes per lb. and 25 minutes over.
Serve veal with bacon rolls and/or sausages, parsley and thyme, or other savoury stuffing, and thickened gravy.
Lemon flavouring blends well with veal, so add a little grated lemon rind and/or juice to the joint during cooking.

Slow roasting:
Less prime joints can be roasted more slowly. Use a very moderate heat, and increase the recommended times by at least 10 minutes per lb. and 10 minutes over.

Accompaniments to Roasts

The various accompaniments that are traditional to serve with roasted meats make them more interesting, and dishes such as stuffings, or Yorkshire pudding, help to make the rather expensive meats used for roasting go further.

Yorkshire Pudding:
The batter as Toad-in-the-Hole, see page 74, makes enough for about 6 people. Make the batter, then heat a knob of cooking fat in an oblong shallow tin, or about 12 small patty tins. Heat the tin(s) in the oven. At this stage I generally increase the oven temperature to very hot, 450–500°F, Mark 8–10. Whisk the batter and pour into the hot tin or tins. Bake

for about 8–10 minutes while the oven is still very hot then reduce to moderately hot again. Allow about 30–35 minutes for the large pudding and about 15–20 minutes for the smaller ones.

Horseradish Sauce:

An economical sauce can be made by adding freshly grated horseradish or the bottled variety to a white sauce, then flavouring this with a little mustard and lemon juice. A richer sauce is made by blending the horseradish into lightly whipped cream, then flavouring the mixture with a little sugar, seasoning, made mustard and enough lemon juice or white vinegar to give a piquant flavour.

Mint Sauce:

Chop fresh mint leaves, add sugar and vinegar to taste. A little boiling water added dissolves the sugar.

Apple Sauce:

Peel and slice good cooking apples, simmer with a small quantity of water, add sugar to taste. If a small knob of butter is added to the sauce it gives a richer flavour. Beat, sieve or emulsify to give a smooth purée. A pinch of mixed spice, ground cinnamon, or ground ginger and dried fruit may be added for extra interest.

Sage and Onion Stuffing:

Peel and chop 2–3 onions. Simmer for 10 minutes only in $\frac{1}{4}$ pint ($\frac{2}{3}$ cup) salted water. Strain and blend with 3 oz. (1 cup) soft breadcrumbs, a little chopped fresh or dried sage and seasoning. Bind with an egg or the onion stock. Cook in, or with the meat.

Veal Stuffing:

This is made as Herb Stuffing, page 28 but add the grated rind and juice of 1 lemon, 2 tablespoons chopped parsley and a little freshly chopped or dried thyme.

BOILED SALT BEEF AND TONGUE

Herb Stuffing:

Adjust the herbs according to the type of meat, e.g. rosemary blends well with lamb, marjoram with veal, sage with pork, and chives with beef. Mix together 4 oz. (2 cups) soft breadcrumbs with 2 oz. ($\frac{1}{3}$ cup) shredded suet, seasoning, 1 egg, grated rind and juice of 1 lemon and about 2 tablespoons chopped herbs. Cook in with the meat or bake in a separate covered dish for 45 minutes. You can add chopped nuts, raisins etc., to the mixture.

TO BOIL MEAT

Let us be clear about the word 'boil'. It is wrong when used to describe the process of cooking various kinds of meat in rapidly boiling liquid (generally water). The liquid should simmer gently; if it boils rapidly then the meat is over-cooked on the outside and becomes dry and hard. Although cured or salted meats are often boiled, you can cook fresh meat in the same way.

Soak salted meat in cold water for at least 12 hours; allow even longer if you are told it is heavily brined or if you wish it to be very mild. Cover the meat with cold water. Throw this away before cooking.

Put the meat into a pan with fresh cold water to cover, or any other liquid, see variations on page 29. Choose a large pan, so the liquid surrounds the meat, for if the meat fits too tightly into the pan, the outside tends to be dry and the meat does not cook as evenly as it should.

Put any vegetables desired, flavouring (herbs etc.) and seasoning with the meat; use pepper or peppercorns with salted meats. Cook for the times given on pages 29–30.

If serving hot lift the meat from the pan with the vegetables, serve with a special sauce or the unthickened liquid. If serving cold allow the meat to cool in the liquid, unless you wish to remove the skin from ham or bacon and sprinkle this with crisp breadcrumbs, or glaze it.

Variations:

Ham in cider: Cover the ham, or bacon with cider and simmer gently. Add small onions and slices of apple towards the end of the cooking time.

Tongue in Ginger ale: Simmer ox, lambs' pigs' or calves tongues in ginger ale or a mixture of ginger ale and water.

Meats to Boil

Beef:
Fresh or salted brisket, silverside, ox tongue, also fresh topside or other joints used for roasting.

Timing Meat: Allow 30 minutes per lb. and 30 minutes over except for the very tender joints, which should have about 20–25 minutes per lb. and 20–25 minutes over.
The beef can be boiled with the various vegetables, such as carrots and turnips and served with small dumplings.

Lamb:
This is not salted. Choose the cheaper pieces of neck of lamb, i.e. middle or scrag end and boil with various vegetables, or use a roasting joint, or tongues.

Timing Meat: Allow 25 minutes per lb. and 25 minutes over for pieces of meat, but when you boil scrag or middle neck with mixed vegetables you should allow a total cooking time of about $1\frac{1}{2}$ hours to make sure the meat is tender. Prime joints, such as leg etc., need the timing above. Boiled lamb is generally served with caper sauce, i.e. white sauce made from milk and the stock in which the lamb is cooked, plus bottled capers and a little liquid from the jar to flavour.

Pork:
Choose head or trotters to make a brawn as the recipe on page 32. Using all trotters makes a cheap, but rather fat brawn; belly, sparerib or loin are good prime cuts to boil, or use pigs' tongues.

Timing Meat: Allow the same time as beef.

Veal:
Choose head to use in a brawn as on page 32, or to serve hot with brain sauce. To make the sauce add the cooked brains from the head to a white sauce. Or choose boned and rolled breast, or tongues.
Timing Meat: As for beef.

Bacon or Ham:
This is cured, however modern methods often produce a mild flavour which does not need soaking. Choose the cheaper forehock, collar, flank for economy; the prime joints – gammon, back and oyster cut – for special occasions.
Timing Meat: 35 minutes per lb. and 35 minutes over for the less tender pieces, but only about 20 minutes per lb. and 20 minutes over for the prime cuts.

COOKING VARIETY MEATS

The variety meats, liver, kidneys, etc., are cooked, as other meats, according to their tenderness. Serve these to your family for they provide iron as well as being good protein foods.

Calves' and lambs' liver can be fried or grilled; since it is a very lean meat I prefer frying, for you can add extra fat to keep it moist. If you add a pinch of sugar to the pan when frying liver you counteract the slight bitterness that children often dislike. Fry slices of orange, apple and bacon with liver too.

Lambs' kidneys should be skinned, halved, coated in seasoned flour and fried or they may be grilled; they are particularly; good on kebabs; keep well basted with butter or oil.

LEMON FLAVOURED LAMBS' BRAWN

Lemon-Flavoured Lamb's Brawn

1 lamb's head
1 or 2 extra lambs' tongues
1 lemon
1–2 leaves

1–2 onions
bouquet garni
2 pig's trotters
seasoning

Wash the lamb's head in plenty of cold water. Put the head, the tongues, thin strips of lemon rind, bay leaves, whole, peeled onions, the bouquet garni (mixed fresh herbs tied in a neat bunch or in muslin), the trotters and seasoning into a large pan. Cover with cold water. Bring slowly to the boil and remove any grey scum from the top of the liquid. Cover the pan and simmer slowly for about 2 hours, or until the meat on the head, tongues and trotters is tender. If preferred cook in a pressure cooker for about 45 minutes at 15 lb. pressure. Drop pressure at room temperature before opening.
Lift the head, tongues and trotters from the liquid and when cool enough to handle, cut all the meat from the bones and arrange in a 3-pint (8 cups) basin or plain mould. Squeeze the lemon juice into the liquid in the pan and boil rapidly until you have about $\frac{3}{4}$ pint (2 cups) liquid left. Strain over the meat in the basin or mould and allow to set.
To turn out, dip the mould for a few seconds in warm water. Invert on to the serving dish and serve with salad.
Serves 8–12 according to the size of the head.

Variation:
Chicken Brawn: Use a boiling fowl or roasting chicken instead of the lamb's head in the recipe above. Joint the chicken and put this into the pan with the rest of the ingredients. Simmer until tender – this will vary with the quality of the bird, but should be about $1\frac{1}{2}$ hours for jointed fowl and 45 minutes or even less for chicken. Remove from the stock, but continue simmering until the trotters are tender, and continue cooking as the basic recipe.

Liver Ragout Sicilienne

$1\frac{1}{4}$ lb. ox-liver
1 oz. ($\frac{1}{4}$ cup) flour
seasoning
3 medium-sized onions
1–2 cloves garlic
2 oz. ($\frac{1}{4}$ cup) dripping or cooking fat
$\frac{1}{2}$ pint ($1\frac{1}{3}$ cups) stock

$\frac{1}{2}$ pint ($1\frac{1}{3}$ cups) cider or inexpensive red wine
a generous tablespoon red currant jelly
$\frac{1}{2}$ teaspoon grated lemon rind
2–3 tablespoons green olives

Cut the liver into narrow strips. Mix the flour with seasoning, coat the liver in this. Cut the peeled onions into rings and crush the cloves of garlic. Heat the dripping or cooking fat in a pan, toss the liver in this, lift out and fry the onion rings and garlic for a few minutes. Gradually blend in the stock and cider or wine, bring to the boil and cook until slightly thickened. Add the jelly and lemon rind. Replace the strips of liver, put a lid on the pan and simmer very slowly for about 2 hours. Add the olives just before serving. Serve with creamed potatoes, boiled rice or noodles.
Serves 4–5.

TO USE THE GRILL

Pre-heat the grill except when cooking gammon (see p. 37).
Brush the food with melted butter or other cooking fat or oil;
this can be flavoured with seasoning, a little lemon juice,
particularly good with veal, a pinch curry powder etc., to
give interest to the meat.
Cook as the timing given on pages 36–37.
Turn the meat with two knives or tongs; do not pierce with
the prongs of a fork, as this allows the meat juices to escape.
Serve as soon as possible after cooking.

Extra Interest to Grilled Foods

Mixed Grill:
Serve small pieces of steak and/or chops, with slices of liver,
bacon, lambs' kidneys, sausages, etc.

Kebabs:
Put diced meat on to metal skewers with mushrooms and
other vegetables and/or fruits, such as prunes, apples. Brush
with melted butter and grill, turning several times.

Add fruit:
Put halved peaches, rings of apple, rings of pineapple etc.
under the grill, brush with butter or oil and cook to serve
with the meat.

CUTS OF MEAT FOR FRYING

Frying and grilling are both rapid methods of cooking and therefore it is essential to choose good quality meats. The reason for frying or grilling rapidly in pre-heated fat, or under a pre-heated grill is to seal the outside of the meat as quickly as possible. These are the cuts to choose:

Beef:
Various steaks, i.e. entrecôte, fillet, minute (very thin slices), rump, point, porterhouse, sirloin, T-bone, Chateaubriand (not suitable for frying).
As beef is a comparatively lean meat, baste well with melted butter when grilling, or be generous with the fat when frying, unless using a non-stick pan, when the amount of fat may be reduced.

Timing Meat:
This applies to both frying and grilling and assumes the steaks are $\frac{1}{2}-\frac{3}{4}$ inch thick.
Under-done (rare): 2–3 minutes on either side.
Medium: 2–3 minutes on either side, then reduce the heat and cook for a further 5–6 minutes.
Well done: 2–3 minutes on either side, then reduce the heat and cook for a further 8–10 minutes (you may like to turn the meat once or twice during cooking).
Minute steaks: 1–2 minutes only on either side.

Lamb or very young mutton:
Choose chops or cutlets from the loin, best end of neck, chump chops (leg chops) and slices from the top of the leg (called fillets).
Lean lamb cutlets or fillets need a reasonable amount of fat.

Timing Meat:
This applies to both frying and grilling and assumes the meat is about $\frac{3}{4}$ inch thick.
2–3 minutes on either side, then reduce the heat and cook for a further 6–8 minutes (you may like to turn the meat once or twice).

Pork:
Choose chops or cutlets from the loin, spare rib, chump (chops only) and slices from the top of the leg (called fillets). Use little, if any, fat for chops, a very small amount for cutlets, but a reasonable amount for fillets.

Timing Meat:
This applies to both frying and grilling, and assumes the meat is about $\frac{3}{4}$ inch thick.
4–5 minutes on either side, then reduce the heat and cook for a further 8–10 minutes. You may like to turn the meat once or twice during cooking.
Note: The fat of pork crisps more readily if it is snipped or cut at $\frac{1}{2}$ inch intervals; the rind should be removed before doing this.

Veal:
Choose chops or cutlets from the loin and slices from the top of the leg (called fillets).
As veal is very lean be generous with the amount of fat used.
Timing Meat: As for pork.

Bacon:
Choose thick slices of mild gammon and prepare and cook as for pork.
It is advisable not to pre-heat the grill and to put the bacon into a cold pan. This prevents the fat curling during cooking.

TO FRY MEAT

Frying in shallow fat is the usual method.
Choose a good-sized solid frying pan; too light a pan is inclined to over-cook the outside of the meat before it is cooked through to the centre.

Fat to choose:
Use butter or cooking fat or oil. The amount must vary according to the quantity of natural fat on the meat. If frying in butter, add a few drops of olive oil – this lessens the possibility of the butter burning and discolouring.
Heat the fat gently until just melted.
Add the meat to the melted fat and cook quickly on one side; turn with tongs or two knives – do not pierce with the prongs of a fork as this allows the meat juices to escape. Fry quickly on the second side, lower the heat if necessary and continue cooking as the timings on pages 36 and 37.
If frying mushrooms and tomatoes as an accompaniment, prepare these and either fry in a separate pan or fry before the meat, if the meat is to be very under-done, then keep the vegetables hot while cooking the meat.
If the meat is to be well cooked, then this may be fried first, lifted on to a hot dish and kept hot while the mushrooms and tomatoes are fried.

Economy hint:
It is possible to save money by using the cheaper meats in various ways:

Austrian Steaks:
Blend 1 lb. (2 cups) minced raw chuck steak with 2 medium grated raw potatoes and 1 medium grated, or minced, raw onion. Flavour with seasoning and mixed herbs. Form into 4–6 round cakes. Coat in a very little seasoned flour, then fry in a small amount of cooking fat for approximately 12 minutes, turning several times. Serve as for steak.

Cider Casserole

4 large onions or 4–5 medium-
   sized leeks
3 oz. ($\frac{3}{8}$ cup) margarine
$\frac{1}{2}$ pint ($1\frac{1}{3}$ cups) cider
seasoning

pinch dried or fresh sage
2–3 dessert apples
4 thick rashers rather fat bacon or
   pork belly

Peel and cut the onions into slices then separate the rings. If
using leeks wash thoroughly and cut into $\frac{1}{2}$-inch lengths.
Heat 2 oz. ($\frac{1}{4}$ cup) of the margarine in a large pan, toss the
onion rings or leek slices in this until a pale golden brown.
Put them into a casserole with the cider, seasoning and herbs.
Cover with a lid and cook for approximately 40 minutes in the
centre of a very moderate to moderate oven, 325–350°F,
Mark 3–4.
Core and slice the apples, but do not peel, and toss in the
remaining margarine. Remove the casserole from the oven,
arrange the apples over the top of the onion and cider mixture.
Top with the uncooked rashers of bacon or pork. Do not put
the lid back on the dish. Return to the oven for a further
25–30 minutes. This is excellent served with baked potatoes.
Serves 4.

Variations:
Use white wine or stock in place of cider.
To make a meal, without using meat, add cooked haricot
beans or a mixture of cooked beans and peas to the onion
mixture with the apples.
Put the apples on top of the onions and cider as detailed in
the recipe. Cover the casserole and cook for 25–30 minutes.
Remove the casserole from the oven and top with fairly thick
slices of Gruyère or Cheddar cheese. Brown under the grill
until the cheese melts, then serve at once.

Beef and Vegetable Stew

1¾ lb. chuck steak
1 oz. (¼ cup) flour
seasoning
8 small or medium-sized onions
8 small carrots
2–3 sticks celery
4 oz. (1 cup) small mushrooms

2 oz. (¼ cup) cooking fat or
 dripping
1 pint (2⅔ cups) brown stock
bouquet garni
Garnish:
chopped parsley

Cut the meat into neat cubes. Blend the flour and seasoning.
Roll the meat in the seasoned flour. Peel the onions and carrots
but leave whole. Cut the celery into neat pieces. Wash the
mushrooms, do not peel.
Heat the fat in a large pan. Toss the onions and meat in this
for a few minutes, turning over and round until the meat is
well coated with the fat. This initial cooking in fat helps to
seal in the flavour of the meat. Stir in the liquid gradually.
Bring the liquid to the boil, stir well until a smooth slightly
thickened sauce. Add the rest of the vegetables, herbs and
season to taste. Cover with a well-fitting lid. Simmer for
2¼–2½ hours.
Serve in a hot dish or casserole. Remove the bouquet garni
and garnish with chopped parsley.
Serves 4–5.

Variations:
The above recipe is a good basis for a variety of different
stews, i.e. replace the vegetables with fruit, such as soaked
prunes; add soaked haricot beans at the beginning of cooking,
and use tomato purée instead of stock or add sliced skinned
tomatoes; blend curry powder, or paprika with the flour.
Turn this recipe into a sweet and sour casserole by blending
a little brown sugar and vinegar into the liquid as it thickens.
Taste and adjust accordingly.

To save time:
Use minced chuck steak; add it to the sauce with the diced
vegetables and cook for only 1–1¼ hours.

Killarney Hot-Pot

8 oz. belly of pork or fairly fat ham
1 lb. lean fresh brisket or best quality chuck steak
1 lb. onions
2–3 large carrots
seasoning
1–2 teaspoons chopped fresh sage or about $\frac{1}{4}$ teaspoon dried sage
$1\frac{1}{2}$ lb. potatoes
$\frac{1}{4}$ pint ($\frac{2}{3}$ cup) brown ale
1 oz. margarine

Cut the meat into neat pieces. Peel and cut the onions and carrots into rings. Season the meat and mix with the sage. Peel and slice the potatoes thinly; keep in water until ready to use, so they do not discolour. Put about one third of the potatoes into the casserole, and season well. Add half the onions and carrots, half the meat, then another layer of potatoes. Save plenty of potatoes for the topping. Season each layer of vegetables. Add the remainder of the meat, onions and carrots and cover with the brown ale. Arrange the last of the potato slices over the vegetables, in a neat overlapping design. Dot small pieces of the margarine on the potatoes. Cook for about 2 hours in the centre of a slow to very moderate oven, 300–325°F, Mark 2–3. Leave the hot-pot uncovered for the first 15 minutes if possible, so the margarine melts and gives a good coating on the potatoes (this stops the lid sticking). Put on the lid after 15 minutes, but remove it again for the last 20 minutes to allow the potatoes to brown and crisp. Serve with cooked red cabbage or pickled red cabbage and apple sauce or sliced cooked beetroot.
Serves 4–5.

Variations:
Choose 2–$2\frac{1}{4}$ lb. jointed middle or scrag end of neck of lamb or mutton instead of the pork and beef.
Add tomato juice or tomato purée instead of the ale.
Children will not dislike the ale in the basic recipe, for its flavour is only pleasantly savoury. Heating always destroys the alcoholic content of beers, wines, spirits.

Corned Beef Plate Tart

Short crust pastry made with
  8 oz. (2 cups) flour, see page 85
Filling:
2 × 12 oz. cans corned beef
2 medium-sized onions
1 tablespoon oil
seasoning
1 teaspoon Tabasco sauce

1 egg
2–3 diced cooked or canned
  carrots
4 oz. (about $\frac{1}{2}$ cup) cooked or
  canned peas
Glaze:
1 egg
Garnish:
parsley

Make the pastry, see page 85 and put on one side. Flake the corned beef and put into a basin. Peel and chop the onions, toss in the hot oil until tender, blend with the corned beef, seasoning, Tabasco sauce, egg and vegetables.
Roll out the pastry, use half to cover a 7–8-inch pie plate or tin. Cover with the filling and the rest of the pastry.
Decorate with leaves of pastry, made from the trimmings. Glaze pastry with the beaten egg. Bake for 25–30 minutes in the centre of a moderately hot to hot oven, 400–425°F, Mark 5–6, then lower the heat to moderate for a further 20–25 minutes. Serve hot or cold, garnished with parsley.
Serves 6.

Note:
As the filling is fairly dry in texture it is not essential to make a slit in the pastry lid.
It is advisable to use a slightly lower oven temperature, and longer cooking time, when you have pastry above and below a substantial filling. This ensures that the bottom pastry sets and browns as well as the top pastry.

Variation:
Milanaise Pie: Omit the cooked or canned carrots and peas and the Tabasco sauce. Blend the beef and onions with 3 skinned chopped tomatoes, 1 tablespoon tomato purée, 2 oz. ($\frac{2}{5}$ cup) cooked rice, seasoning and 1 egg. Bake as recipe above.

Following page: CORNED BEEF PLATE TART *(Photograph by Tabasco Sauc*

Steak and Kidney Pudding

Filling:
1½ lb. stewing steak, chuck is a
  good choice
8–12 oz. ox kidney or 6 lambs'
  kidneys
seasoning
2–2½ tablespoons flour

1 or 2 onions (optional)
water or stock
Pastry:
10 oz. (2½ cups) flour*
pinch salt
5 oz. (nearly 1 cup) shredded suet
water

*This can be self-raising, or plain flour with 2½ level teaspoons baking powder to give a thicker crust, or plain flour for a thin crust that does not rise.

Cut the steak into either neat cubes or narrow strips. Dice the kidney, remove any gristle and skin. Either mix with the meat or put a small piece of kidney on each strip of steak and roll up firmly. Mix the seasoning and flour on a plate or in a bag, turn or toss the meat and kidney in this until evenly coated. Chop the onions finely, if adding these, and blend with the meat. Put the liquid on one side to add later.

Sieve the flour and salt together, add the suet and mix to a soft rolling consistency with cold water. Roll out and use about ¾ to line a 3-pint (8 cups) basin; trim the edges, put trimmings with the ¼ reserved. Put in the meat filling, add just enough water or stock to come halfway up the meat mixture. Damp the edges of the pastry. Roll out the remaining dough to form the lid, put on top of the meat filling, pressing the edges firmly together. Cover with greased greaseproof paper and foil; make a pleat in the centre to allow the pudding to rise.

Either put the basin into a steamer over a pan of boiling water, or lower into a saucepan of boiling water; stand it on an upturned saucer or patty tin. Steam or boil for 4–5 hours so the meat is tender.

Serve in the basin. Make a gravy to serve with the pudding, or when you cut out the first portion add a little good hot beef stock to the filling and use this as the gravy.

Serves 6–7.

Preceding page: STEAK AND KIDNEY PUDDING

FOR SPECIAL OCCASIONS

The meat dishes and methods of cooking meat on the preceding pages can be adapted to give you interesting meals for a special occasion. Here are some ideas to try:
Based upon roasted meats:
Roast the meats in the method described on pages 21–25, but add the following party touches:

(a) Serve roast beef with a mushroom sauce made by simmering 1 lb. (4 cups) button mushrooms in 1 pint ($2\frac{2}{3}$ cups) beef stock, then adding $\frac{1}{4}$ pint ($\frac{2}{3}$ cup) sherry or red wine blended with 2 oz. ($\frac{1}{2}$ cup) flour. Thicken over a low heat, then blend in 2 oz. ($\frac{1}{4}$ cup) butter and season well.
Sauce serves 6–8.

(b) Serve a roasted young leg of lamb with a cherry sauce. Blend $\frac{3}{4}$ pint (2 cups) stock from lamb bones with $1\frac{1}{2}$ oz. ($\frac{3}{8}$ cup) flour. Put into a saucepan and stir until thickened, then add a large can of cherries, all the liquid, $\frac{1}{4}$ pint ($\frac{2}{3}$ cup) port or red wine, seasoning and 1 oz. butter or lamb fat. Heat well, then add a little chopped mint.
Sauce serves 6–8.

(c) Blend roasted veal with a soured cream sauce. Heat 2 oz. ($\frac{1}{4}$ cup) butter or chicken fat in a pan, stir in 2 oz. ($\frac{1}{2}$ cup) flour and cook gently, stirring well. Blend in $\frac{1}{2}$ pint ($1\frac{1}{4}$ cups) veal stock, $\frac{1}{4}$ pint ($\frac{2}{3}$ cup) milk, $\frac{1}{2}$ pint ($1\frac{1}{4}$ cups) dairy soured cream or fresh single (light) cream with up to 2 tablespoons lemon juice. Heat gently, stirring well, until thickened, then add 2 tablespoons capers, a little chopped parsley and the grated rind of 1 lemon. Add a few tablespoons of diced

cooked ham just before serving. Slice the veal, arrange on a hot dish, top with the sauce and garnish with bacon rolls and wedges of lemon.
Sauce serves 6–8.

(d) Serve roasted pork with a sweet-sour sauce. Blend $\frac{1}{4}$ pint ($\frac{2}{3}$ cup) syrup from a medium-sized can of halved apricots with $\frac{1}{2}$ pint ($1\frac{1}{3}$ cups) white stock, 2 tablespoons vinegar, 1 oz. ($\frac{1}{4}$ cup) cornflour, 1 tablespoon brown sugar and 2 tablespoons sweet sherry. Stir over a low heat until thickened, add the quartered apricots and 3 tablespoons tiny cocktail onions.
Sauce serves 8–10.

(e) Roast a chicken as the temperature and directions for beef given on page 22 allowing 15 minutes per lb. and 15 minutes over; (weigh the bird after stuffing). Keep chicken well basted with butter or other fat during cooking so it does not dry. Usually chicken is served with bacon rolls, sausages and bread sauce with a veal stuffing, see page 26, but the following Oriental Sauce is a delicious alternative to gravy: Fry 2 medium onions, chopped finely, and 2 crushed cloves garlic in 3 oz. (3 cups) butter or chicken fat. Blend in 2 oz. ($\frac{1}{2}$ cup) flour, mixed with 1 teaspoon curry powder, a shake of cayenne pepper and a pinch chilli powder (this is very hot). Gradually add 1 pint ($2\frac{2}{3}$ cups) chicken stock. Bring to the boil, season well, lower the heat and add $\frac{1}{4}$ pint ($\frac{2}{3}$ cup) thick cream, 2 tablespoons sherry and 2 tablespoons blanched almonds. Heat gently, do not boil.
Sauce serves 6–8.

Based on frying or grilling.

(a) **Steaks with pâté**: Fry or grill steaks and top with pâté just before serving.

(b) **Hawaiian lamb**: Grill lamb chops or cutlets. Add rings of canned pineapple towards the end of the cooking time. Brush the pineapple with melted butter and sprinkle with a little

48

ground ginger. Heat the syrup from the canned pineapple with finely chopped preserved ginger and pour over the lamb just before serving.

(c) **Gruyère Veal**: Fry fillets of veal in hot butter. Lift on to a flame-proof serving dish. Top with slices of Gruyère cheese. Brown under the grill.

(d) Fry pork chops or cutlets. Lift from the pan and keep hot. Add $\frac{1}{4}$ pint ($\frac{2}{3}$ cup) canned or fresh orange juice, 1 tablespoon honey, 1 teaspoon made mustard to the meat juices in the pan. Heat and spoon over the pork.
Sauce serves 4.

(e) Fry portions of uncoated chicken in hot butter until tender. Lift out of the pan and keep hot. Add $\frac{1}{4}$ pint ($\frac{2}{3}$ cup) red wine, 2 teaspoons chopped fresh basil or $\frac{1}{2}$ teaspoon dried basil to the meat juices in the pan. Heat and pour over the portions of chicken.
Sauce serves 4.

Based upon boiled meats:
Cook chicken, topside of beef, or other prime joints in a mixture of wine and stock. See times on pages 29 and 30.

Chicken Espagnole

8 joints young chicken
1 oz. (¼ cup) flour
seasoning
2 oz. (¼ cup) butter
1 tablespoon olive oil
2 large onions or about 8 small
  onions
1–2 cloves garlic

1 lb. tomatoes
½ pint (1⅓ cups) chicken stock, or
  water and a chicken stock cube
4 oz. (1 cup) small mushrooms
Garnish:
chopped parsley

Wash and dry the chicken, roll in flour, blended with a generous amount of seasoning. Heat the butter and oil in a pan, toss the chicken in this until golden brown. Put it on a plate, and then toss the thinly sliced or whole onions in the remaining butter and oil for 5 minutes. If you like a strong garlic flavour, crush the cloves of garlic and fry with the onions; if you do not like this flavour to be too strong, add the whole cloves of garlic with the onions but remove after 2–3 minutes.

Skin the tomatoes, chop, if very large, and add to the onions, together with the stock, or water and stock cube. Bring to the boil. Add the mushrooms and season well. Put the chicken joints into the pan, but keep them above the level of the liquid if possible. If you like plenty of sauce cover the pan, so the liquid does not evaporate. If you prefer dishes less moist, then leave the lid off the pan for the last 15 minutes. Cook over a low heat for 30–35 minutes. Serve topped with chopped parsley. If preferred, transfer the mixture to a casserole to cook. Cover and allow about 45 minutes to 1 hour in a very moderate to moderate oven, 325–350°F, Mark 3–4. **Serves 4 generous portions.**

Variation:
Add 1–2 sliced green or red peppers to the ingredients above. If you wish the peppers to remain fairly firm in texture add them to the pan or casserole about 10 minutes before the chicken is cooked.

50

Vegetable Dishes

Vegetables are one of the important foods in a family diet. While most people enjoy vegetables (with perhaps one or two exceptions), you may have members of your family who dislike them very much. If they do not like cooked vegetables, they may be persuaded to eat interesting salads. If they dislike green vegetables (an important source of Vitamin C) then make certain they have generous amounts of fresh orange juice, grapefruit and other citrus fruits to compensate.

Cauliflower with Brown Sauce Topping

1 cauliflower
salt
Sauce:
vegetable stock
tomato juice

1 oz. butter or margarine
1 oz. ($\frac{1}{4}$ cup) flour
little yeast extract
Topping:
chopped parsley

Wash the cauliflower, divide into small sprigs and cook in boiling, salted water. Strain after cooking and keep warm. Make the sauce: measure the vegetable stock and add enough tomato juice to give just over $\frac{1}{2}$ pint ($1\frac{1}{3}$ cups). Heat the butter or margarine, stir in the flour and cook for several minutes. Gradually blend in the liquid, bring to the boil and stir well as the mixture thickens. Add enough yeast extract to give a fairly pronounced flavour. Spoon the sauce over the cooked, strained cauliflower and top with chopped parsley.
Serves 4.

52

Cabbage Pancakes

1 very small green cabbage, or
  use the tender outer leaves of a
  large cabbage and save the
  heart for another occasion
seasoning
Batter:
4 oz. (1 cup) plain flour

pinch salt
1 egg
$\frac{1}{2}$ pint ($1\frac{1}{3}$ cups) milk and water
oil or cooking fat for frying
Topping:
4 oz. (1 cup) button mushrooms
little butter

Shred the cabbage and cook very lightly; season well.
Meanwhile make a pancake batter with the flour, salt, egg and
milk and water (see page 71). Strain the cabbage and mix with
the batter. Heat a little oil or cooking fat in a pan and pour
enough of the mixture into the pan to give a thin coating.
Cook until golden brown on the underside, turn and cook on
the second side. Continue to make the rest of the pancakes.
Meanwhile grill or fry the mushrooms in the butter. Serve on
top of the pancakes.
Serves 4–6.

Russian Cabbage:
Mix lightly cooked red or green cabbage with fried onion and
fried apple.

Bubble and Squeak:
This well known dish, famous for using up left-over green
vegetables, is so much nicer if freshly cooked green
vegetables are well drained, tossed in margarine, blended with
mashed potato and seasoning then formed into a smooth
mixture and fried in a little hot butter, margarine or cooking
fat until crisp and golden brown.
Mix cooked green vegetables with:
(a) Soured cream, or thick cream and lemon juice.
(b) Grated nutmeg and lightly cooked carrots and crisply
fried pieces of bacon.
(c) Lightly cooked or raw diced celeriac (celery root) or celery,
melted butter and sultanas.

Boston Baked Beans

1 lb. dried haricot beans	seasoning
water to cover	12 oz. fat salt pork
2 large tomatoes	1–2 onions
1–2 tablespoons black treacle	**Garnish:**
1–2 teaspoons made mustard	parsley

Soak the beans overnight in cold water to cover. Simmer without seasoning in the water for 10–15 minutes. Strain the beans, but save a generous $\frac{1}{2}$ pint ($1\frac{1}{3}$ cups) of the liquid. Simmer this with the tomatoes to make a thin sauce. Sieve. Add the treacle (molasses) and mustard and a generous amount of seasoning.

Dice the pork, peel and slice the onions very thinly. Put the beans, pork and onions into a deep casserole. Pour over the tomato sauce and mix well. Allow plenty of space for the beans to swell during cooking. Put on the lid. Cover very tightly. If the lid does not fit well, put foil round the dish. Cook in the centre of a very slow oven, 250–275°F, Mark $\frac{1}{2}$–1, for about 5 hours.

Check the progress of the cooking after $2\frac{1}{2}$ hours. If the beans are still very hard, raise the temperature slightly. If they are becoming a little dry, add boiling water to moisten, but do not make them too wet. Top with parsley before serving. These can be served as a dish by themselves or as an accompaniment. **Serves about 8.**

Variations:

Omit the pork and add 1–2 crushed cloves of garlic with the tomato mixture.

The tomatoes can be omitted and a little more black treacle (molasses) and mustard used for flavouring.

Children generally love baked beans and it does not matter if they are freshly cooked, as above, or the canned variety. Beans are pulse vegetables, which give protein, so add them to stews and casseroles if you are short of meat.

Top cooked beans with cheese, or serve with cooked fish, bacon, sausages and eggs, etc.

Stuffed Onions

4 large onions
8–12 oz. cooked meat
3 oz. ($\frac{3}{8}$ cup) margarine, butter or
  cooking fat
3 oz. ($1\frac{1}{2}$ cups) soft breadcrumbs

$\frac{1}{2}$ teaspoon chopped fresh sage,
  or good pinch dried sage
2–3 teaspoons chopped parsley
seasoning

Peel the onions. Dice or mince the meat and blend with half
the melted margarine, butter or cooking fat, the crumbs,
herbs and seasoning.
Put the onions into a pan of boiling water, season well and
boil steadily for approximately 30 minutes, until the outsides
are tender. Save some stock to make a sauce if wished. Lift
onions out of the water, cool sufficiently to handle, then
remove the centre of each onion. Chop the centre fairly
coarsely and mix with the rest of the stuffing ingredients.
Brush the bottom of an oven-proof dish or baking tin with
some of the melted fat and put the onion shells on the dish.
Spoon the mixture into the onions, piling it high to give an
attractive appearance. Pour the rest of the melted fat over the
top. Bake in the centre of a very moderate to moderate oven,
325–350°F, Mark 3–4, for approximately 1 hour. If the
stuffing is becoming too brown, cover the dish with foil or a
lid. Serve hot with a sauce if wished.
Serves 4.

Variations:
Use the basic recipe to stuff courgettes. Split the vegetables
lengthways. Simmer in salted water for 10 minutes. Remove
the centre pulp, chop and blend with the mixture, and
continue cooking as the basic recipe for 30 minutes only.
Green peppers are equally good with this stuffing. Cut the
ends from the peppers, remove the core and seeds without
spoiling the shells. Cook these and the slices removed for 6–8
minutes in boiling salted water. Drain and fill with the meat
mixture, put back the slices and cook as the basic recipe for
35 minutes only.

Some ways of cooking Potatoes

Cheese and Potato Bake:
Blend 1 lb. (2 cups) mashed potatoes with 6 tablespoons milk,
1 oz. margarine, 4 oz. (1 cup) grated cheese and 1 egg. Press
into an oven-proof dish. Top with grated cheese and bake for
about 25 minutes towards the top of a moderately hot oven,
375–400°F, Mark 5–6. Serve with meat, fish or egg dishes.
You can add slices of fried sausage or cooked bacon.

Snow-topped Stuffed Potatoes
Halve 4 jacket potatoes when cooked, scoop out the pulp,
mash and mix with 1 oz. margarine, 3 egg yolks, a little
grated cheese, or sliced fried mushrooms, or diced cooked
ham, etc. Press back into the potato halves. Whisk the 3 egg
whites until stiff, fold in seasoning and 2 tablespoons grated
Parmesan cheese. Pile on top of the potatoes and heat for 10
minutes in a very moderate oven, 325–350°F, Mark 3–4.

Potato Nests

1 lb. (2 cups) mashed potatoes
2 oz. ($\frac{1}{4}$ cup) butter
1–2 egg yolks
Filling:
$\frac{1}{2}$ pint ($1\frac{1}{3}$ cups) soured cream or
   yogurt

2–3 tablespoons cooked sweet corn
8 oz. cooked chicken, or diced
   cheese
1 red pepper
seasoning

To the mashed potatoes add the butter and egg yolks. Form
into 6 individual flan shapes or nests. Brown and heat in a
moderately hot oven, 400°F, Mark 6. Meanwhile put the
soured cream or yogurt, sweet corn and chicken or cheese into
the top of a double saucepan, or a basin over hot water. Heat
thoroughly. Add the diced red pepper (discard core and seeds)
and seasoning just before serving. Spoon into the centre of the
crisp potato nests.
Serves 6.

Cheese Dishes

Never waste any little pieces of cheese. If these are of the cooking variety, i.e. Cheddar, Cheshire, Lancashire (this is not as good as the other two), Gruyère, Emmenthal, or the Dutch Edam or Gouda etc., then grate or shred finely and use in cooking. If the cheese is of a type that does not cook well, then dice and mix with salad ingredients or use as sandwich fillings.

Cheese Cups

Cut thin slices of fresh bread, butter generously. Grease patty tins with butter and press the bread into these, buttered side uppermost. Sprinkle with grated Parmesan or other cooking cheese, and bake for about 10 minutes towards the top of a moderately hot oven, 375–400°F, Mark 5–6. Serve hot or cold filled with cooked vegetables or fish or meat in a sauce or gravy. Do not fill until ready to serve.

Cheese Ramekins

Beat together $\frac{1}{2}$ oz. ($\frac{1}{8}$ cup) flour (plain or self raising), 1 oz. butter, 2 tablespoons thin or thick cream, 4 eggs, 4–6 oz. ($1-1\frac{1}{2}$ cups) finely grated Cheddar or other cooking cheese – do not use all Parmesan, as it is too strong. Spoon into greased individual oven-proof dishes and bake for 15 minutes above the centre of a moderately hot oven, 375–400°F, Mark 5–6.

Cheese Salad Dressing

Blend yogurt or mayonnaise, depending on whether you wish a light or rich salad dressing, with grated or crumbled cheese – any type will do. Serve over salads.

Creamy Cheese Spread

Mix 6 oz. (1½ cups) grated or crumbled cheese, it need not be the cooking variety – any cheeses are excellent in this spread, with 1 oz. butter or margarine and enough thick cream, about 4 tablespoons (nearly ½ cup), to make a spreading consistency. Flavour with curry powder, or paprika, or lemon juice, or chopped herbs. Serve on bread or biscuits.

CHEESE SAUCE

A cheese sauce, poured over cooked vegetables, can turn these into a really sustaining dish, It also helps to make small quantities of meat and fish go further. You are giving the family protein, from the milk and cheese, as well as calcium from the cheese. The basic recipe is on page 64, but this can be varied in several ways:
Infuse onion, celery, crushed garlic in the milk for a short time, then strain and use. Use less milk and a little thin cream. Use Gruyère or Parmesan cheeses instead of Cheddar.

USING LEFT-OVER CHEESE

Cheese Soup

Fry 1–2 chopped onions in 2 oz. (¼ cup) butter or margarine until just soft but not coloured. Stir in a generous 1 oz. (¼ cup) flour and cook for several minutes. Gradually blend in ¾ pint (2 cups) chicken stock, or water and a chicken stock cube, and ¼ pint (⅔ cup) milk. Stir until the mixture thickens slightly. Season well and add approximately 4 oz. (about 1 cup) grated cooking cheese. Heat only until the cheese has melted, then serve.

59

Variations:
Cream of Onion and Cheese: Increase the onions to 3. Cut into thin rings, fry in the butter or margarine. Proceed as the basic recipe but add about $\frac{1}{4}$ pint ($\frac{2}{3}$ cup) thick cream before adding the cheese.

Vegetable and Cheese Soup: Use a little more stock and cook about 8 oz. (2 cups) diced vegetables in the sauce mixture before adding the cheese.

Spaghetti Italienne

8–10 oz. spaghetti	8 oz. bacon rashers
seasoning	grated cheese,
large can tomatoes	preferably Parmesan

Put the spaghetti into rapidly boiling, salted water. Use a large pan and at least 4–5 pints of water, so the spaghetti moves freely in the water. Meanwhile put the tomatoes into another pan and heat with plenty of seasoning. Grill or fry the bacon, cut into pieces, add half to the tomatoes. Drain the spaghetti, top with the tomato bacon sauce, the rest of the crisp bacon and grated cheese.
Serves 4–6.

Variations:
Add chopped onion to the tomatoes. Cook sausages, slice and add half to the sauce and top the dish with sausages and bacon. Use cooked ham in place of the bacon.

Savoury Snow Eggs

4 thick slices Gruyère or
   Cheddar cheese
little made mustard
4 slices cooked ham
4 eggs

seasoning
Garnish:
paprika
chopped parsley

Put the cheese into a shallow oven-proof dish. Spread with
the mustard and top with the ham. Put into a moderate to
moderately hot oven, 375–400°F, Mark 5–6 for about
10 minutes.
Meanwhile, separate the egg yolks and whites. Beat the yolks
with seasoning, pour over the ham and cheese. Bake for
5 minutes. Whisk the egg whites until very stiff, add
seasoning and pile over the egg yolk mixture. Return to the
oven, lower the heat to very moderate, 325–350°F, Mark 3–4,
and leave for about 10–15 minutes. Garnish with paprika and
chopped parsley.
Serves 4.

Savoury Supper Rice

2 oz. margarine
4 oz. (1 cup) small mushrooms
4 large tomatoes

1 large onion
8 oz. ($1\frac{1}{3}$ cups) long grain rice
1 pint ($2\frac{2}{3}$ cups) water, or stock
seasoning
grated cheese, optional

Heat the margarine in the pan and toss the whole mushrooms,
peeled sliced tomatoes and onion in this for a few minutes.
Add the rice, and turn in the vegetable mixture, then pour in
the water or stock. Bring to the boil, add seasoning and cook
steadily for approximately 25 minutes until the rice is tender
and the excess liquid absorbed. Pile on to a hot dish and top
with the grated cheese.
Serves 4–6.

Onion and Cheese Flan

Pastry:
6 oz. (1½ cups) flour, preferably
  plain
good pinch salt
shake pepper
pinch dry mustard
pinch cayenne pepper
3 oz. (⅜ cup) margarine or butter
1 oz. (⅛ cup) grated Parmesan
  cheese
1 egg yolk and water to bind

Filling:
2 large onions
little water
seasoning
1 level tablespoon cornflour
¼ pint (⅔ cup) milk
2 eggs
2 tablespoons cream
4 oz. (1 cup) grated Cheddar or
  Gruyère cheese

Sieve the flour and seasonings together. Rub in the margarine or butter, add the cheese, then bind with the egg yolk and water. Roll out and line an 8-inch tin or flan ring or dish. Bake blind in a moderately hot oven, 400°F, Mark 5–6, until quite cooked.

Meanwhile cook the neatly sliced onions in just enough water to cover. Season, cover the pan tightly, so the liquid does not evaporate. When the onions are cooked, blend the cornflour with the milk, add to the onions and liquid and cook steadily until thickened. Remove the pan from the heat. Blend the beaten eggs with the cream, stir into the onion mixture and cook without boiling for about 3 minutes. Add the cheese and heat until melted. If serving the flan hot, put the hot filling into the hot pastry and serve as soon as possible. If serving the flan cold, allow the filling and pastry to cool, then put the filling into the flan case.

Serves 4–5.

Variation:
Use 2 oz. (½ cup) grated Cheddar or Gruyère cheese in place of the Parmesan cheese; since these are less dry I would use about ½ oz. less margarine or butter in the pastry.

This cheese pastry flan case can be baked blind and used as the basis for many savoury dishes:

Fill with white or cheese sauce, blended with cooked vegetables, flaked cooked white fish, or chicken.

Cheese Caesar Salad

2–3 slices of bread
little butter or oil
8 oz. cheese, any kind or use a
  mixture of cheeses

2–3 hard boiled eggs
mayonnaise
little Worcestershire sauce
lettuce

Remove the crusts from the bread, cut into neat croûtons and
fry in the hot butter or oil until crisp and golden brown,
drain very well on absorbent paper. Dice or crumble the
cheese and mix with the sliced eggs and mayonnaise, flavour
with a few drops of Worcestershire sauce. Arrange the
shredded lettuce in a bowl, toss in seasoned oil and vinegar if
wished. Top with the cheese and egg mixture and add the
croûtons of bread just before serving.
Serves 4–5.

Variations:
This salad is a splendid basis for other dishes:
Use flaked fish instead of diced cheese; you can top the salad
with a little more mayonnaise and grated cheese. Use diced
ham with the eggs instead of cheese and arrange well-drained
cooked prunes on the shredded lettuce. For a luxury touch
garnish with anchovy fillets, which blend well with cheese
or ham as well as fish.
Children generally enjoy the unexpected crispness of this
salad.

Economy hint:
You can use left-over pieces of cheese, that may have become
a little dry; let them stand in the mayonnaise for a while
before completing the salad.

To save time:
Cook a good supply of croûtons and keep these in an airtight
container in a cool place or freeze them; they can be separated
as and when required and just warmed through in the oven,
then allowed to cool.

Vegetable Cheese Pie

2 oz. ($\frac{1}{4}$ cup) butter or margarine
4 large tomatoes
2 onions
2 oz. ($\frac{1}{2}$ cup) mushrooms
small can asparagus tips
seasoning
12 oz. ($1\frac{1}{2}$ cups) mashed potatoes

Cheese sauce:
1 oz. butter or margarine
1 oz. ($\frac{1}{4}$ cup) flour
$\frac{1}{2}$ pint ($1\frac{1}{3}$ cups) milk
4 oz. (1 cup) grated Cheddar cheese
Garnish:
1–2 tomatoes

Heat 1 oz. butter or margarine and fry the skinned chopped tomatoes, onions and mushrooms until softened. Mix with the drained asparagus tips and seasoning. Spoon into 4 individual dishes.

Add the rest of the butter or margarine to the potatoes and season. Put into a piping bag with a $\frac{1}{4}$-inch rose pipe (icing nozzle) and pipe a border round the edge of the dishes.

Make the cheese sauce as below. Spoon over the vegetables. Brown under the grill or in the oven, and serve at once, garnished with sliced tomato.

Serves 4.

Variations:
Use flaked cooked fish instead of the selection of vegetables.
Use one vegetable only instead of the selection in the recipe.

Cheese Sauce

Choose a good cooking cheese – Cheddar, Gruyère, Dutch, etc. or Parmesan. Grate, shred or chop this. Heat 1 oz. butter or margarine, stir in 1 oz. flour, blend in $\frac{1}{2}$ pint ($1\frac{1}{3}$ cups) milk (for a coating sauce). Stir until thickened, season – add made mustard and cayenne pepper as well as salt and pepper – add the cheese, heat gently, but do not over-cook, otherwise the sauce curdles. Allow 4–6 oz. ($1–1\frac{1}{2}$ cups) Cheddar or similar cheese but half the quantity of stronger Parmesan cheese.

Serves 4.

64

Salads

A salad meal is ideal for light luncheon or supper and the ideas on this and the next few pages can be adapted, according to the season, to serve your family. Do not be too conservative in your choice of salad ingredients; if lettuce is not obtainable, or is very expensive, remember that cabbage or other greens, such as Brussels sprouts, spinach, etc., are delicious if they are shredded finely. Endive is another green salad vegetable that is often neglected.
Use fruits in salads in addition to, or instead of, the usual tomatoes, cucumber, etc.

Cheese, Bacon and Potato Salad

Dice cheese neatly, fry several chopped rashers of bacon and mix with cooked, diced potatoes while the bacon is still hot. Allow to cool, then blend with a very little mayonnaise plus a dash of vinegar or lemon juice, to counteract the richness of the bacon. Serve on a bed of green lettuce, or an alternative, such as watercress, and garnish with sliced raw mushrooms, sliced tomatoes and cucumber.

Chef's Salad

This is a splendid way of using any small amounts of various meats. Take any meats available – a good combination is tongue, ham, chicken and beef – and cut into matchstick pieces. Cut any cheese, Gruyère is best for this purpose, into similar sticks. Mix lightly with mayonnaise, or a little oil and vinegar, and season well. Make a bed of mixed salad in a bowl, top with the meat and cheese mixture, and garnish with chopped nuts.

Tuna Salad

Flake tuna fish, and mix with mayonnaise, diced cucumber, or gherkins when cucumber is expensive, and coarsely chopped hard boiled eggs. Arrange in a ring of watercress or shredded green lettuce or other greens. Top with more chopped hard boiled egg. Canned salmon or cooked white fish may be used instead of tuna, but flavour the mayonnaise with either a little anchovy essence, or tomato purée, or ketchup.

Savoury Tongue Salad

Tongue is a fairly expensive meat so make it go further in the following way:
Blend diced green pepper (discard the core and seeds) and equal quantities of a fairly sweet pickle and mayonnaise. Spread over slices of cooked tongue. Roll lightly and arrange on a bed of mixed salad.

Coleslaw

Never worry unduly if your children do not like cooked cabbage, serve it raw (when it retains the maximum of mineral salts and vitamins) in a cabbage salad – generally called a coleslaw. Remember, prolonged soaking allows these precious salts and vitamins to be wasted so do not prepare too long before serving.

heart of a small white cabbage	1 tablespoon vinegar and
3 large carrots	mayonnaise to taste
	little chopped parsley

Wash, dry and shred the cabbage very finely. Grate the peeled carrots. Put into a bowl with the cabbage, then add the vinegar and enough mayonnaise to bind. Add a little chopped parsley to the salad and top with extra parsley just before serving.
Serves 6–8.

Variations:
The above recipe is a very ordinary coleslaw, but it looks attractive with the pale green and golden colour of the carrots. Make the salad more exciting in the following ways.

Savoury Coleslaw:
Blend a pinch of curry powder, pinch of ground ginger and/or ground cinnamon with the mayonnaise before adding to the cabbage and carrots. Add a small amount of chopped nuts and raisins too, or capers and sliced gherkins.

Apple Celery Coleslaw:
Omit the carrot and blend finely chopped dessert apple and diced celery with the cabbage. Toss the apple in the vinegar, or use lemon juice instead, before mixing with the rest of the ingredients. Add a little dried fruit too.

Main dish coleslaw:
Make the basic recipe or any of the variations and blend sliced hard boiled eggs, diced cooked ham or chicken with the various ingredients. If you take the heart from the cabbage very carefully, so you leave an attractive outer shell, you can pile the salad back into this.

Children's Coleslaw:
Make this as the main dish coleslaw but use sliced sausages, baked beans in tomato sauce. The moisture from the tomato sauce means you could reduce the mayonnaise, which many children dislike.

Grapefruit Jellied Salad

2 grapefruit
$\frac{1}{4}$ pint ($\frac{2}{3}$ cup) thick mayonnaise
$\frac{1}{2}$ oz. gelatine
$\frac{1}{2}$ pint ($1\frac{1}{3}$ cups) tomato juice

8 oz. cooked lean ham, cut in
  1 thick slice if possible
seasoning
mixed salad

Halve one grapefruit and squeeze out all the juice, make up to $\frac{1}{4}$ pint ($\frac{2}{3}$ cup) with water. Halve the other grapefruit and spoon out the segments carefully discarding pips and skin, blend these with the mayonnaise.

Soften the gelatine in a little cold tomato juice then dissolve in the remaining hot tomato juice. Allow to cool, then blend with the grapefruit juice. Leave until the mixture just starts to stiffen slightly, then fold in the grapefruit and mayonnaise and the neatly diced ham. Taste the mixture and add seasoning if required, some people may like a little sugar. Put into an oiled $1\frac{1}{2}$–2 pint (4–$5\frac{1}{3}$ cups) mould and leave until firm. Turn out on to a bed of mixed salad.
Serves 4–6.

Note:

If the mayonnaise is not very thick, then use 2 tablespoons less tomato juice, or less water, when diluting the grapefruit juice.

Variations:

Use the grapefruit salad above and add whole or chopped prawns in place of the ham.

Use 2–3 pineapple rings instead of the grapefruit segments and pineapple syrup instead of grapefruit juice. This makes a sweeter salad, which also blends well with ham or lean cooked pork.

If using canned grapefruit use the syrup plus a squeeze of lemon juice to sharpen this.

Slimmers should use yogurt in place of mayonnaise.

Children may enjoy the refreshing flavour of this salad but it is generally a more adult taste.

Egg Dishes

An egg supplies both protein and iron to the diet, and not only makes a good breakfast dish, but can be used as the basis of many light supper or luncheon meals.

If eggs, as a complete dish, are not popular with any members of your family then use them in cooking, so you make sure the family are getting their food value, which is not spoiled in cooking. For example, add an egg, or egg yolk, to mashed vegetables; whisk an egg into a white sauce, after it has boiled and thickened; mix short crust pastry with an egg instead of water; home-made cakes generally make good use of eggs.

Scotch Eggs

4 eggs
little flour
seasoning
12 oz.–1 lb. (1½–2 cups) sausagemeat

Coating:
1 egg
2–3 tablespoons crisp breadcrumbs
cooking fat or oil for frying

Hard boil the eggs, cool and shell. Coat each egg in a little seasoned flour – this makes the sausagemeat stick round the egg better.

Divide the sausagemeat into four portions, press out into neat squares on a floured board. Wrap round the eggs, then seal the ends and roll until neat shapes. Coat with beaten egg and crumbs. These may be fried in deep cooking fat or oil, in which case turn once to brown and fry for about 5–6 minutes. If using shallow cooking fat or oil, then turn several times and cook for about 10–12 minutes. Remember, it is essential to ensure that the sausagemeat is thoroughly cooked. If preferred, bake for about 25 minutes in the centre of a moderate to moderately hot oven, 375–400°F, Mark 5–6. Serve hot or cold.
Serves 4.

Pancakes

Batter:
4 oz. (1 cup) flour, preferably
   plain
pinch salt
1 egg

$\frac{1}{2}$ pint ($1\frac{1}{3}$ cups) milk, or milk and
   water
oil or cooking fat for frying

Sieve the flour and salt, add the egg and a little milk, or milk and water. Beat or whisk thoroughly to give a smooth thick batter. Gradually whisk in the rest of the liquid.

For each pancake you cook, put about 2 teaspoons oil or a knob of cooking fat the size of an unshelled almond into the pan. If using a non-stick pan then brush with oil or melted cooking fat before cooking each pancake. This is essential if you want really crisp pancakes. Heat the oil or cooking fat until a faint blue haze is seen coming from the pan. Pour or spoon in a little batter, then move the pan so the batter flows over the bottom, it should give a paper thin layer. Cook fairly quickly until set on the bottom. This takes about $1\frac{1}{2}$–2 minutes. To test if ready to toss or turn, shake the pan and the pancake should move easily if cooked on the under surface. Toss or turn carefully. Cook for about the same time on the second side. Lift or slide the pancake out of the pan. Keep hot while cooking the rest of the pancakes.

This batter should give enough pancakes for 4 people, but you may be able to serve more if using a substantial filling.

As a sweet:
Serve with sugar and slices of lemon or orange; fill with hot jam; fill with hot or cold cooked or raw fruit; fill with ice cream; pour melted chocolate over each pancake.

As a savoury:
Sprinkle with grated cheese; fill or top with cheese sauce; fill with cooked vegetables (blended with a sauce if wished); fill with fried bacon and tomatoes or mushrooms; fill with cooked meat or poultry or fish tossed in butter.

Savoury Pancake Boat

Batter:
4 oz. (1 cup) flour, preferably plain
pinch salt
1 egg
$\frac{1}{2}$ pint (1$\frac{1}{3}$ cups) milk, or milk and water
1 oz. cooking fat
3–4 hard boiled eggs
3 oz. ($\frac{3}{8}$ cup) butter or margarine
2 oz. ($\frac{1}{2}$ cup) flour

$\frac{1}{2}$ pint (1$\frac{1}{3}$ cups) chicken stock
$\frac{1}{4}$ pint ($\frac{2}{3}$ cup) milk
seasoning
about 4–6 oz. ($\frac{1}{2}$–$\frac{3}{4}$ cup) diced cooked chicken
2–3 tablespoons thin cream
2–4 oz. ($\frac{1}{2}$–1 cup) button mushrooms
chopped parsley
Garnish:
sprigs of watercress

Make the batter as pancakes, see page 71. Heat the cooking fat in a shallow tin, pour in the batter and bake for approximately 25–30 minutes towards the top of a hot to very hot oven, 450–475°F, Mark 7–8. Reduce the heat after about 15 minutes to moderate.

Meanwhile slice the eggs. Make a sauce with 2 oz. ($\frac{1}{4}$ cup) of the butter or margarine, the flour, chicken stock and milk. When thickened and smooth, add the seasoning, chicken and cream; do not allow to boil.

Heat the remainder of the butter or margarine, fry the whole or sliced mushrooms. Add most of the sliced eggs and mushrooms to the chicken mixture. Lift the batter from the tin on to a hot serving dish, spoon the sauce mixture over this. Top with the remainder of the eggs, mushrooms and chopped parsley. Garnish with watercress.
Serves about 6.

To save time:
Make the batter as the recipe. Heat a small amount of cooking fat in individual patty tins. Pour in the batter, cook for about 15 minutes only. Top with the chicken mixture.

Economy hint:
This is an excellent way of using small pieces of left-over chicken; meat or fish could be used instead.

Toad-in-the-Hole

Batter:
4 oz. (1 cup) flour, preferably
  plain
pinch salt
2 eggs

$\frac{1}{4}$ pint ($\frac{2}{3}$ cup) milk
6 tablespoons water
$\frac{1}{2}$ tablespoon oil, or melted butter
1 oz. dripping or cooking fat
1 lb. sausages

Sieve the flour and salt, add the eggs and the milk and beat hard to make a smooth thick batter. Gradually whisk in the water and allow to stand until nearly ready to cook, then whisk in the oil or melted butter, this gives an added crispness to the batter.

Heat the dripping or cooking fat for a few minutes in a shallow oven-proof dish or tin, then add the sausages and cook for nearly 10 minutes in the centre of a hot oven. Raise the heat to very hot, 450–475°F, Mark 7–8, then pour the batter over the hot sausages. Cook for 10 minutes then lower the temperature to moderately hot and continue cooking until the batter is crisp and golden; the time varies with the depth of the mixture but should be about 20–25 minutes after lowering the heat. Serve at once.

Serves 4–6.

Variations:

Use the slightly different batter for pancakes on page 71. You may find that this method of serving sausages is very popular with children. It can be adapted in many ways. Use halved kidneys or strips of lambs' or calves' liver or small chops or cutlets in place of sausages: add halved tomatoes to the meat; blend 2–3 oz. ($\frac{1}{2}$–$\frac{3}{4}$ cup) grated Cheddar cheese with the batter.

When cooking fairly fat chops to serve this way omit the 1 oz. dripping or cooking fat; simply cook the meat to extract some of the fat before adding the batter.

Plain Omelette

2 or 3 eggs
seasoning
1 tablespoon water
1 oz. butter

filling or flavouring, see individual
recipes

Beat the eggs, seasoning and water lightly. I use a fork only for a plain omelette like this, for I find over-beating gives a less moist result.

Heat the butter in the omelette pan, make quite sure it is hot, but do not let it darken in colour, otherwise it spoils the look of the omelette. Pour the eggs into the hot butter then wait $\frac{1}{2}$–1 minute until the eggs have set in a thin film at the bottom. Hold the handle of the omelette pan quite firmly in one hand, then loosen the egg mixture from the sides of the pan with a knife and tilt the pan slightly; the pan should be kept over the heat all this time. This is known as working the omelette and it allows the liquid egg from the top of the mixture to flow to the sides of the pan and cook quickly. Continue tilting the pan, loosening the sides and moving the mixture until it is as set as you like. People vary considerably in the way they like their omelettes cooked, some prefer them just set, others like them fairly liquid in the centre.

Add any filling mentioned in the recipe. Fold or roll the omelette away from the handle of the pan. Hold the pan firmly by the handle, then tip the cooked omelette on to a very hot serving dish or plate. Garnish as liked and serve at once.

Serves 1 person as a main course.

Fillings:
Fill the omelette with grated cheese, flaked cooked fish or shellfish, tossed in butter or mixed with a thick sauce; diced ham, diced chicken, tossed in butter or thick cream or blended with a thick sauce; cooked asparagus, mushrooms, tomatoes or other vegetables make excellent fillings.

Desserts

The desserts that follow incorporate many favourite dishes, with suggestions for new ways of serving these.

Baked Egg Custard

1 pint (2⅔ cups) milk
2 eggs

1 oz. (⅛ cup) sugar
nutmeg

Heat the milk but do not let it boil; it should be about blood temperature. Beat the eggs and sugar together, then add the hot milk, stirring all the time.
Strain into a greased pie dish, grate a little nutmeg on top. Stand the dish in a bain-marie, i.e. another dish containing cold water. Bake in the coolest part of a slow oven, 275–300°F Mark 1–2, for approximately 45 minutes to 1 hour until the mixture is set.
Serve in the pie dish. It is not sufficiently firm to turn out. This can be a pudding by itself or it can be served with cooked fruit.
Serves 4–5.

Children often dislike plain egg custards and the Fruit Queen of Puddings recipe on page 90 is one way to make the basic recipe more exciting.
Try topping a baked custard with a layer of strawberry jam then whipped cream and grated chocolate.

Ice Creams

Modern commercial ice cream forms the basis of an excellent dessert, but you can make your own quickly and easily. The first recipe is a very economical one and the variations cover ways to make it richer and to incorporate eggs, etc.

large can unsweetened
   evaporated milk
1 teaspoon gelatine (optional)

2 oz. ($\frac{3}{8}$ cup) sieved icing sugar
   flavouring, see recipe

Although you can use evaporated milk straight from the can it is better to boil it, for this makes it whip more readily and gives a whiter mixture (providing you do not boil it for too long a period), also a much lighter textured ice cream. Put the can of evaporated milk into a saucepan with plenty of water and boil steadily for 15 minutes, no more. Remove from the water and open the can carefully as the hot milk tends to spurt out.

Meanwhile soften the gelatine in a tablespoon cold water, stir into the very hot milk and continue stirring until dissolved. If you omit the gelatine the mixture does not hold its shape quite as well.

Chill the milk, then whisk until light and fluffy, then fold in the sugar and any flavouring. Spoon into the freezing trays or utensil and freeze as rapidly as possible. There is no need to whisk the mixture during freezing.

Serves 4–6.

Simple flavourings: Blend any essences (vanilla, rum, etc.,) with the mixture. Blend instant coffee powder with some of the milk; do not use liquid coffee.

Blend in sieved chocolate or cocoa powder. Add $\frac{1}{4}$ pint ($\frac{2}{3}$ cup) thick fruit purée.

Variations:

Make $\frac{1}{2}$ pint ($1\frac{1}{3}$ cups) custard with 2 egg yolks, 1 oz. ($\frac{1}{8}$ cup) sugar and $\frac{1}{2}$ pint ($1\frac{1}{3}$ cups) milk. Cool and blend with the evaporated milk. Freeze for 35 minutes, then fold in the 2 stiffly whisked egg whites and re-freeze.

Use a mixture of thick and thin creams in place of evaporated milk, whip the thick cream then gradually whisk in thin cream.

Iced Lollies

These can be made with ice cream (use the recipe on page 77) or make more refreshing 'lollies' with fruit juice or fruit purée. Although fruit squash, etc. could be used, fresh fruit juice (orange in particular) is excellent for children, as it provides them with Vitamin C.
The special moulds in which to freeze lollies are quite inexpensive and should last indefinitely.

Orange Lollies

Squeeze the juice from oranges or rub the pulp through a sieve or emulsify in the liquidizer to give a smooth purée. To save money the juice or purée can be diluted with a little water or you can simmer the peel with water (for additional flavour) for 5 minutes. Try to avoid using any sugar in sweetening the orange juice or purée – or use the minimum, so that children do not develop a taste for over-sweet foods. Pour or spoon the juice or purée into the moulds and freeze until very hard – the 'stick' should be placed into position before freezing.
Other fruit juices to use: diluted rose hip syrup, blackcurrant syrup (well diluted), grapefruit, pineapple juice.

Apple Lollies

Simmer apples with a very little water and sugar or honey to taste. The fruit may be flavoured with a little lemon juice. Emulsify or sieve to make a very smooth purée, then freeze in the moulds. Tint a pale green if wished.
These lollies can be made by half filling the moulds with apple purée (coloured with a very few drops of green – do not over-colour), then freezing until firm. Chilled orange juice is then poured into the half filled moulds and the lollies are frozen until both layers are firm.
Other fruit purées to use: sieved fresh raspberries, strawberries, black and red currants, cooked plums.

Baked Apples

4 medium-sized to large cooking
  apples

approximately 1 tablespoon brown
  or white sugar

Core the apples; do this either with an apple corer or a
pointed knife. In order to prevent the skin bursting during
cooking make a light slit round the centre of the apples. Put
the apples into an oven-proof dish, fill the centres with sugar.
Bake for approximately 1 hour in the centre of a moderate
oven, 350–375°F, Mark 4–5, or allow 15 minutes longer in a
very moderate oven, 325°F, Mark 2–3. The skin may be left
on the apples. Serve with custard sauce, cream, or ice cream.
Serves 4.

Variation:
Baked Apples with Orange Filling: Ingredients as for baked
apples minus the sugar, plus 2–3 tablespoons of orange
marmalade, the finely grated rind of 1–2 oranges and
approximately 2 tablespoons orange juice. Blend the
marmalade, grated rind and juice and put into the apples
before cooking.
While the apples are cooking, cut neat pieces of orange
segments. Remove the apples from the oven a few minutes
before serving, spoon the orange segments on top, return to
the oven to heat; or omit orange pieces and decorate with
strips of rind.

Baked Oranges

4 large oranges
1 oz. butter

2 oz. (good $\frac{1}{2}$ cup) brown sugar
3 tablespoons rum

Try and choose the seedless variety of orange. Cut away the
peel and also the outer pith. Cut the oranges across the centre
and put into a lightly buttered dish, with the cut sides
uppermost. Top with brown sugar, rum and rest of the butter.
Bake for 20–25 minutes in a moderate oven, 350–375°F,
Mark 4–5.
Serves 4.

Following page: BAKED APPLES WITH ORANGE FILLING

Gooseberry Sparkle

1 packet lime or other flavoured
  jelly
1 medium can gooseberries

Decoration:
whipped cream
chopped glacé cherries
chopped crystallized ginger

Read the instructions on the packet for the exact amount of
water or liquid required; this varies slightly according to
different makes. Strain off the syrup from the can of fruit and
dilute with water to make up to the quantity given on the
packet less about 1 tablespoon. This is because the fruit is
moist and will dilute the strength of the jelly.
Dissolve the jelly according to the instructions. Pour a little
into a rinsed mould. Allow this to become nearly set and
arrange the first layer of fruit on top. It is easier to do this
if you dip the fruit in liquid jelly. When set pour over a little
more jelly and continue filling the mould like this to give an
interesting design. Allow to set and turn out. Decorate with
the whipped cream, chopped glacé cherries and chopped
crystallized ginger.
Serves 4.

Variations:
Use other flavoured jellies and fruits in the same way.
Harlequin Jelly: Omit the fruit and use water plus a little
fresh orange or lemon juice to give the quantity recommended
on the packet. When the jelly is cold and just beginning to
stiffen add the following: 3 tablespoons of diced glacé
cherries, 2 tablespoons raisins or sultanas, 2 tablespoons
quartered marshmallows and 2 tablespoons coarsely chopped
walnuts. Stir into the jelly and put into a mould, rinsed in
cold water, allow to set.
Milk Jelly: Take any fruit flavoured jelly and dissolve in
$\frac{1}{4}$ pint ($\frac{2}{3}$ cup) very hot water. When this is cold add $\frac{3}{4}$ pint
(2 cups) cold milk, or milk and thin cream. Allow to set.

Preceding page: GOOSEBERRY SPARKLE *(Photograph by Cadbury Schweppes Food Advisory
Service, Bournville, Birmingham, England)*

FRUIT FLANS

*These are some of the most delicious of all desserts. Choose really crisp
pastry, the recipe below is ideal, and take care when filling this to arrange
the fruit carefully so the completed flan looks as good as it will taste.*

Fleur Pastry

3 oz. ($\frac{3}{8}$ cup) butter or best
    quality margarine
2 oz. ($\frac{1}{4}$ cup) castor sugar
1 egg yolk

6 oz. ($1\frac{1}{2}$ cups) flour, preferably
    plain
little cold water

Cream the butter or margarine and sugar until soft and light.
Beat in the egg yolk, add the sieved flour, blend with a
palette knife. Gradually stir in enough water to bind. Roll
out in to a circle about 10 inches in diameter (this makes an
8-inch flan or pie case).
If using a shallow tin grease lightly. If using a flan ring stand
on an upturned baking tray or sheet.
Put the rolling pin under the pastry to support it, then lower
into the case. Slip the rolling pin away as you do so. Press
the pastry into the case with your fingers. Either cut away
any surplus pastry with a sharp knife, or take the rolling pin
backwards and forwards over the pastry.
To keep the flan case a perfect shape it should be weighted
to prevent the pastry base rising and the sides losing their
shape; this is called 'baking blind'. Either prick the base of
the flan case, put in a double thickness of foil and press
firmly against the pastry, or grease a round of greaseproof
paper lightly and place greased side downwards into the flan
case. Fill with dried haricot beans or crusts of bread. Bake in
the centre of a moderate to moderately hot oven, 375–400°F,
Mark 5–6, for 15–20 minutes, or until the pastry is just set.
Remove the foil, or paper and beans, or bread, then continue
baking for 5–10 minutes until golden brown. Lift away the
flan ring and if the pastry is a little pale return to the oven
for a few minutes. Cool slightly, put on to a wire cooling tray.
When cold fill and glaze.

To fill the flan:
You will need about 1 lb. of fruit. This can be cooked, canned, or frozen. The latter should be almost defrosted. Drain the fruit carefully through a sieve, retain the syrup. It spoils the appearance and taste of ripe cherries, raspberries and strawberries if they are poached in syrup. Make a syrup from sugar and water, use 2–4 oz. ($\frac{1}{4}$–$\frac{1}{2}$ cup) sugar to each $\frac{1}{4}$ pint ($\frac{2}{3}$ cup) water. Put the fruit into the syrup while it is still warm. Leave for 2–3 minutes, lift out the fruit, strain as above. Put the drained fruit into the flan case carefully.

To make the glaze:
If the flan case is fairly shallow use $\frac{1}{4}$ pint ($\frac{2}{3}$ cup) syrup, but if it is fairly deep, use $\frac{1}{2}$ pint (1$\frac{1}{3}$ cups). Blend the syrup with 1 or 2 teaspoons (nearly 2$\frac{1}{2}$ teaspoons) arrowroot or cornflour. Put into the saucepan, stir well, cook until thickened. Add a few drops of colouring if necessary, or about 2 tablespoons redcurrant jelly, or sieved raspberry jam for extra flavour. When thickened and clear, cool but do not allow to set. Brush or spread over the fruit.

Serves 6.

Variations:
In all of these recipes the flan case should be baked.

Banana Coconut Flan:
Mash 4 bananas with 2 tablespoons lemon juice and 2 tablespoons sugar. Add 4 tablespoons desiccated coconut. Stand for 20 minutes then gradually beat in $\frac{1}{2}$ pint (1$\frac{1}{3}$ cups) thick cream. Fill the flan and top with a little toasted coconut and glacé cherries.

Hawaiian Chiffon Pie:
Dissolve $\frac{1}{2}$ oz. gelatine in $\frac{1}{4}$ pint ($\frac{2}{3}$ cup) syrup from canned pineapple. Add $\frac{1}{2}$ pint (1$\frac{1}{4}$ cups) finely chopped pineapple, mix with the gelatine and allow to stiffen lightly. Fold in $\frac{1}{4}$ pint ($\frac{2}{3}$ cup) lightly whipped cream; whisk 2 egg whites and fold in 2 oz. ($\frac{1}{4}$ cup) sugar and blend with the pineapple mixture. Fill the flan, leave until firm then decorate with angelica and pineapple pieces.
Use other fruits instead of pineapple.

Short Crust Pastry

8 oz. (2 cups) flour, preferably   4 oz. ($\frac{1}{2}$ cup) fat*
  plain   cold water to mix
pinch salt

*This can be cooking fat, margarine, butter or a mixture of these fats.
All cooking fat gives a very crisp crumbly pastry, and you may like to
use $3\frac{1}{2}$ oz. (just under $\frac{1}{2}$ cup) only

Sieve the flour and salt. Cut the fat into convenient-sized
pieces, drop into the bowl. Rub in with the tips of your
fingers until the mixture looks like fine breadcrumbs. Do not
overhandle. Lift the flour and fat as you rub them together so
you incorporate as much air as possible and keep the mixture
cool. Gradually add the water to give enough moisture to bind
the ingredients together. Use a palette knife to blend. Flour
varies a great deal in the amount of liquid it absorbs, but you
should require about 2 tablespoons water. When blended,
form into a neat ball of dough with your fingers. Put on to a
lightly floured pastry board, and roll out to a neat oblong or
round about $\frac{1}{4}$ inch in thickness unless the recipe states to the
contrary. Always roll in one direction and do not turn the
rolling pin; instead, lift and turn the pastry. This makes sure
it is not stretched badly.
Cook as the individual recipes; generally short crust pastry
needs a hot oven to set the pastry, but you may need to reduce
the heat after a time.

Quick Ways to Use Short Crust Pastry

Jam Tarts:
Roll out the pastry, line patty tins. Put in a little jam, bake for 12 minutes above the centre of a hot oven, 425–450°F, Mark 7–8. Top with a little more jam the moment the tarts come from the oven.

Puff Pastry

The method of rolling and folding is similar to flaky pastry, see page 102. Sieve 8 oz. (2 cups) plain flour with a pinch of salt, bind with a squeeze of lemon juice and water. Roll out to an oblong. Place 8 oz. (1 cup) butter, or other kind of fat, in the centre of the dough. Fold to cover the butter. Turn and proceed as flaky pastry, see page 102, but give 7 rollings and 7 foldings.

Lemon Meringue Pie

Fleur pastry with 6 oz. (1½ cups) flour, etc., see page 83
2 lemons
water
1 oz. butter
2½ tablespoons (generous ¼ cup) cornflour
4–8 oz. (½–1 cup) castor sugar, see method
2 eggs

Make the flan case and bake blind, see page 83. Grate the top rind from the lemons, squeeze out juice, measure and add water to give ½ pint (1⅓ cups). Blend the cornflour with the lemon juice and water, put into a pan with the grated rind, 2–4 oz. (¼–½ cup) sugar, depending on whether you like a sharp or sweet flavour, and the butter. Stir over a gentle heat until thickened. Remove from the heat, separate the eggs, and add the beaten yolks. Return to the heat and cook gently for several minutes. Taste, add even more sugar if wished. Spoon into the pastry case.

Whisk the egg whites until very stiff, add 2–4 oz. (¼–½ cup) sugar. There are several ways of incorporating the sugar. The best way is gradually to beat in half the sugar, then fold in the remainder gently and slowly. A softer meringue is given, if you gradually fold in all the sugar, and a very firm meringue, only successful if you have a mixer, is obtained if you gradually beat in all the sugar. Spoon the meringue over the lemon mixture, so it touches the pastry rim.

To serve freshly cooked use the smaller quantity of sugar if desired. Brown for 20 minutes in the centre of a very moderate oven, 325–350°F, Mark 3–4, or 5–8 minutes in a hot oven.

To serve cold use full proportions of sugar. Bake for at least 1 hour in the centre of a very slow to slow oven, 225–250°F, Mark ½–1.

Variation:

Use other fruits – tangerines are delicious.

Following page: LEMON MERINGUE PIE

Fruit Queen of Puddings

2 tablespoons jam
2 oz. soft breadcrumbs
2 eggs
¾ pint (2 cups) milk

3 oz. (⅜ cup) castor sugar
3 tablespoons diced fresh or
   canned fruit

Spread half the jam in an oven-proof dish. Add the crumbs. Separate the egg yolks and make the custard using the yolks, milk and 1 oz. (⅛ cup) sugar. Pour over the crumbs and bake as for Baked Egg Custard, page 76, until firm. Spread with the jam and most of the fruit. Whip egg whites until very stiff, fold in remaining sugar. Pile on to the custard and top with the remaining fruit. Bake for 15 minutes in a moderate oven, 375°F, Mark 4–5. Serve hot.
Serves 4.

Lemon Cheese Tart

Short crust pastry made with
  6 oz. (1½ cups) flour, etc.
1 lemon

8 oz. (1 cup) cream cheese
2 eggs
2 oz. (¼ cup) sugar

Roll out the pastry and line an 8-inch pie plate. Bake blind as the flan on page 83, in a hot oven for 15 minutes only. Mix the grated rind and juice of the lemon with the cream cheese, beaten eggs and sugar. Spoon into the pastry case, return to the oven, lowering the heat to very moderate, 325–350°F, Mark 3–4, and continue baking for a further 25 minutes until firm and golden. Serve cold.
Serves 4–6.

Preceding page: FRUIT QUEEN OF PUDDINGS

Apple Raisin Turnovers

short crust pastry, made with
  6 oz. (1½ cups) flour, etc.
3 large cooking apples

3 oz. (½ cup) raisins
2 tablespoons sugar
1 tablespoon apricot jam

Roll out the pastry and cut into 4 rounds. Peel and slice the apples, mix with the raisins and sugar and jam. Cover half the pastry squares with the apple mixture. Damp the edges of the pastry and fold over to make half circles. Press the edges firmly. Lift on to baking trays and cook for 15 minutes in the centre of a hot oven, 425–450°F, Mark 6–7, then lower the heat to moderate and continue cooking for a further 10–12 minutes. Serve hot or cold.

Variations:
Pineapple and Mincemeat Turnovers:
Fill the turnovers with 6 oz. (1 cup) mincemeat and 5 tablespoons chopped well-drained canned pineapple.
Banana Apple Turnovers:
Fill the turnovers with the 3 sliced apples blended with 2 mashed bananas, 2 oz. (¼ cup) sugar and 1 tablespoon lemon juice.
Cheese and Apricot Turnovers:
Fill the turnovers with 6 oz. (¾ cup) cream cheese or grated cheese blended with 1½ tablespoons thick cream and 3 tablespoons apricot jam.

Fruit Crumble

1–1¼ lb. prepared fruit
little water
sugar to taste

*can be plain or self-raising

Crumble:
4 oz. (1 cup) flour*
2 oz. (¼ cup) butter or margarine
2–3 oz. (¼–⅓ cup) sugar

Put the fruit into a pie or oven-proof dish. If cooking soft berry fruit use no water or about 1 tablespoon if very firm; with harder fruit use 3–4 tablespoons water. Add sugar to sweeten. Cook gently in the oven for 10–15 minutes. If you prefer berry fruit to be firm, do not cook this before adding the crumble topping. Sieve the flour, rub in the butter or margarine, add the sugar. Sprinkle over the top of the fruit. Bake in the centre of a moderate oven, 350–375°F, Mark 4–5, for 25–30 minutes until crisp and golden brown.
Serve in the baking dish, with cream or custard sauce. It is nicer served hot rather then cold.

Variations:
Sift ½–1 teaspoon ground ginger, cinnamon or other spice with the flour, or add the grated rind of 1 or 2 oranges or lemons. You can use the same flavourings in the charlotte, see page 95, and either mix with the crumbs and sugar or sprinkle over the fingers of bread, after frying.
If children like nuts, sprinkle a thin layer of chopped nuts over the crumble just before the end of the cooking time. Slimmers should avoid the top crumble mixture and just eat the fruit.

To save time:
Make up a large quantity of crumble and store in polythene bags or containers in the refrigerator or freezer, or use the canned fruit pie fillings, or ready cooked fruit.

Nut and Pineapple Upside Down Cake

Topping:
2 oz. ($\frac{1}{4}$ cup) butter
2 oz. ($\frac{1}{2}$ cup) brown sugar
few canned pineapple rings
few pecan, or halved walnuts
few Maraschino cherries

Sponge:
5 oz. ($\frac{5}{8}$ cup) butter or margarine
5 oz. ($\frac{5}{8}$ cup) sugar
2 eggs
6 oz. ($1\frac{1}{2}$ cups) self-raising flour,
    or plain flour and $1\frac{1}{2}$ level
    teaspoons baking powder
few drops vanilla essence
3 tablespoons milk

To make the topping: melt the butter in a 7–8-inch cake tin or oven-proof dish, cover with the brown sugar. Arrange a design of pineapple rings, pecan, or halved walnuts, and Maraschino cherries on the butter and sugar.

To make the sponge mixture: cream together the butter or margarine and sugar until soft and light. Whisk the eggs well and beat gradually into the butter mixture. Sieve the flour or flour and baking powder, mix the vanilla essence and milk. Fold the flour and milk alternately into the creamed mixture. Pour the sponge mixture over the topping and bake in the centre of a very moderate oven, 325–350°F, Mark 3–4, for about 1 hour. Turn out, serve hot or cold with cream, as a dessert or for a cake.

Serves 4–6.

Variations:
Peel and core apples, cut into rings and use instead of pine-apple rings. Dip the apple rings in lemon juice before putting on top of the butter and sugar mixture. Use halved canned pears, or peaches, or apricots.

The sponge topping may be flavoured in many ways: Sieve 1–2 teaspoons ground ginger or other spice with the flour. This is particularly good with pears and apples. Use 3 tablespoons strong coffee in place of milk and use this over an apricot base.

Fruit Charlotte or Brown Betty

1–1¼ lb. prepared fruit
little water
sugar to taste

Charlotte mixture:
4–5 large slices bread
3 oz. (⅜ cup) butter or margarine
2 oz. (¼ cup) sugar (preferably brown)

If using firm fruit, such as apples, plums, etc., cook in a covered saucepan with a little water and sugar to taste until softened. Berry fruits (such as raspberries, loganberries, etc.) may also be cooked first, but if you prefer these to remain firm then do not cook.

There are two ways of making a charlotte. The first is to remove the crusts and then cut the bread into neat fingers. The second method is to make fairly coarse crumbs from the bread. Heat the butter or margarine in a large frying pan and fry the bread in this until just golden coloured. Put one third of the bread slices or crumbs into a pie or oven-proof dish, sprinkle with some of the sugar. Add half the fruit. If using uncooked soft fruit sprinkle with sugar. Put a second layer of bread and a sprinkling of sugar, then the rest of the fruit, or uncooked fruit and sugar. Top with an even layer of bread and sugar. Bake for about 35–40 minutes in the centre of a moderate oven, 350–375°F, Mark 4–5.

Serve in the dish or invert this on to a hot serving plate and decorate with cooked or raw fruit.

Serves 4–6.

Variation:
Substitute 4–5 oz. (3–3¾ cups) cornflakes for the breadcrumbs. Toss the cornflakes lightly in the hot butter or margarine then mix with the sugar. Bake as above.

Economy Hint:
The method of using bread, as in this recipe, produces a very economical and satisfying dessert.

Following page: CORNFLAKE BROWN BETTY

Home Baking

The art of home baking is one that gives a great deal of satisfaction to the cook and pleasure to her family and friends. While too many cakes, cookies, etc., do not constitute a well balanced diet, a reasonable amount of these foods help to provide interesting and varied meals. You will find it considerably cheaper to make cakes and bread yourself, rather than buying them, and it gives you an opportunity to incorporate really nutritious ingredients.

Yeast Cookery:

Bread and buns with yeast are inexpensive to make, so if you have a family of growing children, with very large appetites, try this form of baking. To begin with you may find it seems a lengthy process, but while the yeast dough is rising you can be doing other jobs in the home.

You can put the dough into the refrigerator to rise overnight, if more convenient. Bring it out the next day, and let it stand at room temperature for a short time, then knead and use as the individual recipe.

Plain Buns

$\frac{1}{2}$ oz. yeast
2 oz. ($\frac{1}{4}$ cup) sugar
just under $\frac{1}{2}$ pint ($1\frac{1}{3}$ cups) tepid
   water or milk

1 lb. (4 cups) plain flour
good pinch salt
1 oz. margarine
1 egg

This is a good starting point for yeast cookery as imperfections of handling are less noticeable than when making bread. You can add fruit to the basic ingredients above or top the cooked buns with some kind of icing or use this for doughnuts. The process of making is as bread, see page 114.

Preceding page: WEINERBRØD AND HOT CROSS BUNS

Weinerbrød Danish Yeast Pastries

$\frac{3}{4}$ oz. yeast
2 oz. ($\frac{1}{4}$ cup) sugar
$\frac{1}{2}$ pint ($1\frac{1}{3}$ cups) tepid milk, or
   milk and water
1 lb. (4 cups) plain flour
6–8 oz. ($\frac{3}{4}$–1 cup) butter or
   margarine
1 egg

Fillings:
(see method)
Icing:
8 oz. ($1\frac{1}{2}$ cups) icing sugar
little water
glacé cherries and/or chopped
   nuts

Cream the yeast with 1 teaspoon of the sugar, add the tepid liquid and a sprinkling of flour. Leave in a warm place for 15–20 minutes until the surface is covered with bubbles. Put the rest of the flour into a bowl. Rub in 2 oz. ($\frac{1}{4}$ cup) butter or margarine, add the rest of the sugar. Divide the remaining butter or margarine into two portions, leave at room temperature to soften. Add the yeast liquid to the flour, stir in the egg. Mix well, turn on to a floured board, knead until smooth. Return to the mixing bowl, cover with a cloth, leave for about 1 hour to rise, i.e. until double its original size. Knead again and roll out to an oblong shape, about $\frac{1}{2}$ inch in thickness. Spread with half the softened butter or margarine, fold in 3, turn at right angles, then roll out once more. Spread with the last of the butter or margarine, fold in 3, turn at right angles, roll again, fold and turn. The dough is now ready to use and can be made into different shapes.

One of the most popular shapes is the envelope. To make these roll out the dough until about $\frac{1}{4}$ inch thick. Cut into 4-inch squares. Put a little filling, i.e. jam, honey, lemon curd, thick apple purée, marzipan or chopped preserved ginger, in the centre of each square. Fold so the corners come to the centre, covering the filling.

Lift the pastries on to warmed flat baking trays. Allow to tise for 20 minutes in a warm place. Bake for approximately 12 minutes above the centre of a hot oven, 425–450°F, Mark 6–7; cool. Blend the icing sugar with enough water to give a thin coating. Spread over each pastry. Top with glacé cherries and/or finely chopped nuts.

Maids of Honour

Puff, flaky or rough puff pastry
  made with 6 oz. (1½ cups) flour,
  etc., see page 102
Filling:
little jam
6 oz. (1 cup) cottage cheese
2 oz. (½ cup) sultanas
½ teaspoon almond essence

2 tablespoons ground or finely
  chopped almonds
2 eggs
Topping:
4 oz. (¾ cup) icing sugar
little water
few drops almond essence

Roll out the pastry until wafer-thin. Cut into 12–15 rounds, to fit into fairly deep patty tins about 3 inches in diameter. When gathering up the pieces lay these carefully one over the other, and re-roll to use for some of the rounds. Do not squeeze into a ball, as this spoils the pastry.

Put a teaspoon of jam into each pastry case. Sieve the cheese, add the other ingredients for the filling and beat well until a smooth mixture. Spoon into the pastry cases and bake for 10 minutes in the centre of a hot to very hot oven, 450–475°F, Mark 7–8. Lower the heat to moderate, 350–375°F, Mark 4–5, and cook for a further 15 minutes, or until both pastry and filling are set. Allow to cool.

Blend the icing sugar with enough water to make a flowing consistency. Add a few drops of almond essence. Spoon a little into the centre of each tartlet and leave to set.
Makes 12–15.

Economy hint:
Use fine, stale cake or biscuit crumbs in place of cottage cheese. This gives a more crumbly texture which is very pleasant.

Flaky Pastry

8 oz. (2 cups) flour, preferably
  plain
pinch salt

6 oz. ($\frac{3}{4}$ cup) butter or other fat*
water to mix, as cold as possible

*A favourite combination is half margarine and half fat

Sieve the flour and salt into a mixing bowl. Rub in one third of the fat. Add enough water to make an elastic dough. Roll out to an oblong on a lightly floured board. Divide the remaining fat in half, if hard soften by pressing with a knife. Put over the top two-thirds of the pastry in small pieces. Bring up the bottom third of the pastry dough and fold like an envelope. Bring down the top third.
Turn the pastry at right angles, seal the ends of the pastry then depress this at regular intervals with a lightly floured rolling pin. This is called 'ribbing' the pastry. Roll the dough out into an oblong shape again. If you find it feels sticky and is difficult to roll then put away in a cool place for another 30 minutes, or longer if wished. Repeat the process described above, using rest of the fat. Roll out to the required shape, chill until ready to use.
Cook as the individual recipe, but flaky pastry needs a hot to very hot oven to encourage the pastry to rise and to prevent it being greasy. Serve hot or cold.

Variation:
Rough Puff Pastry: Use the same proportions of fat as for Flaky Pastry, but put this into the flour and salt. Cut into tiny pieces and blend with water, or water and a squeeze of lemon juice. Roll out to an oblong shape, fold as for flaky pastry and continue the method of rolling. Allow 5 rollings and 5 foldings in all.

Having made or bought the frozen, or packet versions of the richer pastries do make use of them in interesting ways. Flaky pastry is an excellent topping for sweet and savoury pies, although I think it better for the latter. Rough puff and puff pastry can be used in the same way.

Doughnuts

bread or bun dough, see
   pages 98 and 114
jam

cooking fat or oil for frying
sugar

Choose the dough you prefer. For round doughnuts roll in
balls and remember those made with yeast dough rise to about
twice the original size. Make a depression with the tip of your
finger or the handle of a spoon and fill with jam, then re-roll
the ball to cover the jam. For ring doughnuts roll out and cut
into rings. Allow yeast doughnuts to rise, see page 99.
Cook in deep cooking fat or oil. Heat oil or cooking fat until
it reaches 370–375°F; a cube of bread should turn golden in
30 seconds. Slide the doughnuts into the hot oil or cooking fat.
Put in as many as you can but allow space between each to
turn them over. Cook quickly until they rise to the surface
and begin to colour underneath, turn carefully and continue
to cook until golden brown all over. Lift out carefully with a
perforated spoon or fish slice. Drain over the pan for a few
seconds, then on absorbent paper. Roll in sugar spread on a
plate, or drop into a bag of sugar and shake vigorously until coated.

Variations:
Spiced Doughnuts: Sieve a little mixed spice with the flour.
Honey Doughnuts: Add 1–2 tablespoons warmed honey to
the yeast mixture before blending with the flour, etc. This
means you should either be more sparing with the liquid or
work in a little extra flour so the mixture may be handled
easily.
Fruit Doughnuts: Add dried fruit to the flour.
Apple Doughnuts: These make a delicious dessert if served
hot. Make very thick apple purée, or use other cooked fruit.
Allow this to cool so it becomes even more solid. Mix with
chopped nuts or dried fruit for extra interest. Make a deep
depression, as described in the basic recipe, put in the fruit
purée, roll the dough round this, and fry as above. Serve hot,
dusted with sugar, and with more hot fruit purée.

Following page: DOUGHNUTS

Economical Dundee Cake

5 oz. ($\frac{5}{8}$ cup) margarine or butter
5 oz. ($\frac{5}{8}$ cup) sugar
2 large eggs
8 oz. (2 cups) self-raising flour, or plain flour with 2 level teaspoons baking power

12 oz. (generous 1$\frac{1}{2}$ cups) mixed dried fruit
2 oz. ($\frac{1}{4}$ cup) glacé cherries
2 oz. ($\frac{1}{2}$ cup) chopped candied peel
little milk
Decoration:
1–2 oz. ($\frac{1}{5}$–$\frac{2}{5}$ cup) blanched almonds

Cream the margarine or butter and sugar together, and gradually beat in the eggs. Fold in the sieved self-raising flour, or plain flour and baking powder gently, then the fruit, cherries and peel, and enough milk to give a soft dropping consistency. Put into a 7–8-inch greased and floured, or lined and greased tin and cover with the almonds. Brush these with a little egg white – there is enough left in the egg shells after making the cake. Bake for about 1$\frac{3}{4}$ hours in the centre of a very moderate oven, 325°F, Mark 3; lower the heat slightly after 45 minutes to 1 hour if the cake becomes too brown. This cake tends to rise in a pleasant round instead of being flat.

Variations:
Spiced Dundee Cake: Sieve 1–2 teaspoons mixed spice with the flour.
Increase the fat and sugar to 6 oz. ($\frac{3}{4}$ cup), the fruit to 1$\frac{1}{2}$ lb. (generous 3 cups), use 4 large eggs and very little milk. Increase the baking time to just over 2 hours, reducing the heat after about 45 minutes.

Note:
The fruit cakes are a splendid stand-by for a family. They keep well so you can make several at one time and store them in well sealed containers.

Almond Cake

6 oz. ($\frac{3}{4}$ cup) margarine or butter
6 oz. ($\frac{3}{4}$ cup) castor sugar
3 large eggs
8 oz. (2 cups) flour*
2 oz. ($\frac{1}{2}$ cup) ground almonds
1 lb. (2 cups – well filled)
   mixed dried fruit

2 oz. ($\frac{1}{4}$ cup) glacé cherries
2 oz. ($\frac{1}{2}$ cups) chopped candied peel
little milk
Decoration:
little egg white or apricot jam
  jam.
1–2 oz. ($\frac{1}{5}$–$\frac{2}{5}$ cup) blanched
  almonds

*Either half self-raising and half plain flour or all plain flour with
1$\frac{1}{2}$ level teaspoons baking powder.

Cream the margarine or butter and sugar together. Gradually
beat in the eggs. Fold in the sieved flour or plain flour and
baking powder gently with the ground almonds, then the
fruit, cherries and peel and just enough milk to make a soft
consistency. Put into a 7–8-inch greased and floured, or lined
and greased tin. Bake for 2–2$\frac{1}{4}$ hours in the centre of a very
moderate oven, 325°F, Mark 3, reducing the heat to slow
after about 1–1$\frac{1}{2}$ hours. When the cake is cooked brush with
a little egg white or apricot jam, and cover with a thick layer
of blanched and flaked almonds and brown for a few minutes
under the grill.

Note:
Do not exceed the amount of baking powder in this recipe
otherwise the fruit could fall to the bottom of the cake in
baking.
This cake should be kept a few days at least before cutting.
It keeps well for some time in a well sealed container.

Variations:
Omit the ground almonds in the cake and substitute an extra
1 oz. ($\frac{1}{4}$ cup) flour.
Omit the dried fruit, cherries and peel and add 4 oz. (1 cup)
ground almonds to the flour to make a delicious moist plain
cake, bake for approximately 1$\frac{1}{2}$ hours.

Scotch Pancakes

4 oz. (1 cup) flour*
pinch salt
1 egg

$\frac{1}{4}$ pint ($\frac{2}{3}$ cup) milk, or milk and
   water
very little fat

*Use either self-raising flour, or plain flour with 1 level teaspoon baking
powder or plain flour with $\frac{1}{4}$ level teaspoon bicarbonate of soda and
$\frac{1}{2}$ level teaspoon cream of tartar

Sieve the self-raising flour, or flour and raising agent, well
with the salt. Add the egg and beat, then gradually whisk in
the milk or milk and water to give a smooth batter.
The old-fashioned griddle, sometimes called a girdle or
bakestone, has become difficult to find, but modern versions
are being made. The alternatives are to use a solid hotplate
on an electric cooker, again becoming less plentiful with
modern-type cookers, or a frying pan. If the frying pan is
heavy then use it in the normal way, but if it is light-weight
the scones are inclined to burn and I find the best thing is to
turn the frying pan upside-down and cook the scones on
the base.
Grease the griddle or substitute and heat. Test by dropping a
teaspoon of the batter mixture on to the warm plate; the
batter should set almost at once and begin to bubble within
1 minute. If this does not happen then heat the griddle a
little longer before cooking the scones.
Drop the scone mixture from a tablespoon on to the griddle
and cook for 1–2 minutes until the top surface is covered with
bubbles. Put a palette knife under the scone and turn
carefully; cook for the same time on the second side. To test
if cooked, press gently with the edge of the knife and if no
batter oozes out then the scones are cooked. Lift on to a clean
teacloth on a wire cooling tray and wrap in the cloth until
ready to serve.
Serve either cold with butter, or warm topped with butter
and jam, or cooked, well drained fruit or syrup, as a quick and
easy dessert. These are also excellent if served with cooked
sausages and beans as a supper snack.
Makes 10–12.

SCOTCH PANCAKES *(Photograph by RHM Foods Limited)*

Hot Cross Buns

generous $\frac{1}{2}$ oz. yeast
3 oz. ($\frac{3}{8}$ cup) sugar
just under $\frac{1}{2}$ pint (generous 1 cup) milk, or milk and water
1 lb. (4 cups) plain flour
pinch salt
$\frac{1}{2}$ teaspoon allspice
$\frac{1}{2}$ teaspoon ground cinnamon
2 oz. ($\frac{1}{4}$ cup) butter or margarine
about 3 oz. ($\frac{1}{2}$ cup) dried fruit
Glaze:
2 oz. ($\frac{1}{4}$ cup) sugar
2 tablespoons hot water

Cream the yeast with a teaspoon of the sugar. Add the milk, or milk and water, together with a sprinkling of flour. Put in a warm place for 15–20 minutes until the surface is covered with bubbles.

Meanwhile sieve the flour, salt and spices together. Rub in the butter or margarine, add the remainder of the sugar, the dried fruit, then the yeast mixture. Knead lightly but well. Cover and leave in a warm place to rise. This takes at least 1 hour. Knead again, cut into 12–16 pieces, form into rounds. Put on to warmed, lightly greased baking trays, mark a cross on each bun with a knife. Leave to rise for about 15 minutes, then bake as the Danish pastries, page 99. Blend the sugar and water. Brush the buns with this glaze as soon as they come from the oven.

Makes 12–16.

Variation:
To make more prominent crosses, pipe on a cross of thick batter before baking.

Baking Powder Doughnuts

8 oz. (2 cups) self-raising flour, or
  plain flour and 2 teaspoons
  baking powder
good pinch salt
1 oz. melted butter or oil
approximately 6–7 tablespoons
  (just over $\frac{1}{2}$ cup) milk or better
  still use milk and water

1 egg
1–2 oz. ($\frac{1}{8}-\frac{1}{4}$ cup) sugar
Filling:
jam, see Doughnuts page 103
oil or cooking fat for frying, see
  Doughnuts page 103
Coating:
sugar, see Doughnuts page 103

Sieve the dry ingredients together. Add the butter or oil, the egg and sugar and mix. Then gradually add enough milk to make a soft rolling or handling dough. If slightly sticky, cover and stand for about 10 minutes. Prepare and cook as Doughnuts, see page 103.
Makes about 8.

Gold Ginger Loaf

10 oz. (2½ cups) plain flour
1 level teaspoon bicarbonate of
  soda
½ teaspoon ground ginger
6 oz. (½ cup) clear honey
4 oz. (½ cup) fat
6 oz. (¾ cup) sugar
2 tablespoons syrup from jar of
  preserved ginger
1½ tablespoons milk
2 eggs
Decoration:
1 tablespoon honey
few leaves angelica
2–3 tablespoons preserved ginger,
  cut in neat pieces

Sieve the dry ingredients into the mixing bowl.
To weigh the honey: Put an empty saucepan on the scales,
note the weight, then add 6 oz. (½ cup) honey, or syrup – see
variation.
To measure the honey: If the measuring cup is floured the
honey, or syrup – see variation – pours out easily into the
saucepan. Add the fat and sugar to honey in the pan. Heat
gently until the fat melts, pour over the flour and beat well.
Warm the ginger syrup and milk in the pan, add to the flour
mixture with the eggs and beat until smooth. Line a 2½–3 lb.
loaf tin with greased greaseproof paper. Pour in the mixture.
Bake in the centre of a slow to very moderate oven,
300–325°F, Mark 2–3, for 1–1¼ hours until just firm to the
touch, do not over-cook. Remove from the oven, cool in the
tin for about 15 minutes. Remove from the tin, take off the
paper, then brush the top with the honey and press the
pieces of angelica and ginger into position.
Serve as a cake with coffee or tea, or spread with butter as a
tea-bread. This is also delicious sliced and topped with apple
purée.

Variation:
To make a darker, stronger flavoured loaf use golden syrup
or black treacle or a mixture of these, in place of the honey.
The amount of ground ginger may be increased to 2 teaspoons,
as the above recipe has a very mild flavour.

112

TO MAKE BREAD

As the process is lengthy, and cooked bread freezes excellently, I have given the recipe based on 3 lb. (12 cups) flour to make several small loaves. If you want to make just one loaf then use 1 lb. (4 cups) flour and reduce all ingredients in proportion, except the yeast. Use $\frac{1}{2}$ oz. fresh yeast or dried yeast in proportion. If you can buy strong flour, you have a better result. Failing this use plain flour.

3 lb. (12 cups) strong flour
   3 teaspoons salt
1 oz. yeast

1 teaspoon sugar
approximately $1\frac{1}{2}$ pints (4 cups)
   tepid water

Sieve the flour and salt into a warm bowl. Cream the yeast with the sugar, add most of the liquid. Make a well in the centre of the bowl of flour, pour in the yeast liquid and sprinkle flour on top. Cover the bowl with a clean cloth and leave for about 20 minutes, until the surface is covered with bubbles. Mix the liquid with the flour, if too dry then add sufficient tepid liquid to give an elastic dough. Turn out of the bowl on to a floured board and knead until smooth. Either put back into the bowl and cover with a cloth or put into a large greased polythene bag. Leave to rise until almost double the original size. Turn on to the board again and knead. Form into the shaped loaves you like; for a tin loaf grease, flour and warm the tins. Form the dough into an oblong shape, fold into three to fit the tin and lower into the tin. The dough should come just over half-way up the tins. If you brush the loaves with a little melted fat or oil it produces an excellent crust. Cover the tins with a cloth or polythene, allow to rise for 20 minutes.

Bake for about 20–25 minutes in the centre of a hot oven, 425–450°F, Mark 6–7, after this lower the heat to very moderate and complete cooking. A 1 lb. (4-cup) tin loaf takes a total of about 35–40 minutes.

To test the bread turn the loaves out of the tins, knock firmly on the base. The bread should sound hollow. If it does not, return to the oven for a little longer.

Makes 3 loaves.

Variations:

Using fat: Rub 2–3 oz. ($\frac{1}{4}$–$\frac{3}{8}$ cup) margarine or other fat into the flour.

Milk loaf: Blend with milk instead of water.

Fruit loaf: Add 6 oz. (1 cup) dried fruit and 2–4 oz. ($\frac{1}{4}$–$\frac{1}{2}$ cup) sugar to the flour. Bake the loaves as the basic recipe. When they come from the oven top with a sugar and water glaze.

To glaze 3 loaves: Blend 2–3 oz. ($\frac{1}{4}$–$\frac{3}{8}$ cup) sugar with 2 tablespoons boiling water. Brush over the bread. The same glaze can be used for topping buns.

Hamburger Rolls: The recipe for bread can be adapted to make the soft hamburger rolls. Be a little more generous with the amount of liquid in the recipe, adding this until you produce a very slightly sticky dough. Knead, as given in the recipe. Allow to rise. Knead again and form into rounds. Put the rolls on to the warmed baking trays, allowing plenty of room for them to spread out, then flatten the rounds slightly with your hands. Allow to rise as for bread, but this takes only approximately 15 minutes with rolls. Bake for 12 minutes towards the top of a very hot oven, 450–500°F, Mark 8–10. 1 lb. (4 cups) flour etc., makes 12–14 large rolls.

Crisp Topped Rolls: Recipe as for bread, but be a little more sparing with the liquid and these are better mixed with milk rather than water, and with a small amount of margarine, or other fat, rubbed into the flour. When the dough has risen form into small rounds, batons or other shapes. Brush with beaten egg then a little melted margarine and allow to rise for approximately 15 minutes, then bake for about 12 minutes towards the top of a very hot oven, 450–500°F, Mark 8–10. 1 lb. (4 cups) flour etc., makes about 18–20 small rolls.

Baking Powder Rolls: Sieve 8 oz. (2 cups) self-raising flour or plain flour with 2 teaspoons baking powder and a good pinch salt. Bind with milk or milk and water to make a slightly sticky dough. Knead lightly for 1 minute on a floured board. Divide into 8 portions, put on an ungreased baking tray and cook as for previous recipe.

Cheese and Date Bread

8 oz. (2 cup) self-raising flour,
  or plain flour and 2 teaspoons
  baking powder
1 level teaspoon dry mustard
seasoning
2 oz. ($\frac{1}{4}$ cup) butter or margarine

4 oz. (1 cup) grated Cheddar,
  Gruyère or Cheshire cheese
2–3 oz. (nearly $\frac{1}{2}$ cup) chopped
  dates
2 eggs
$\frac{1}{4}$ pint ($\frac{2}{3}$ cup) milk or buttermilk

Sieve the flour, or the flour and baking powder, and the
seasonings. Rub in the butter or margarine, add the cheese
and dates, 1 whole beaten egg and nearly all the second egg,
saving 1 good teaspoon to brush the top of the loaf. Add the
milk or butter milk and beat well.
Grease and flour a $1\frac{1}{2}$–2 lb. loaf tin. Put in the mixture, brush
with the beaten egg. Bake for 45–50 minutes in the centre of
a moderate oven, 350–375°F, Mark 4–5, until quite firm to
the touch. Lower the heat after 30 minutes to very moderate,
if the loaf is browning too much. Slice and butter. Serve fresh,
either hot or cold.

Variation:
The above gives a fairly shallow loaf. If preferred, bake in a
1 lb. loaf tin for about 1 hour.
Children will enjoy this and it is a splendid way of
incorporating protein into the diet.

MAKING COOKIES

Cookies (or biscuits) are an ideal stand-by, for they keep almost indefinitely if stored in an air-tight tin, away from cakes, bread and biscuits.

Chocolate Date Cookies

4 oz. ($\frac{1}{2}$ cup) butter
4 oz. (generous $\frac{1}{2}$ cup) brown
  sugar
6 oz. ($1\frac{1}{2}$ cups) self-raising flour*

1 oz. ($\frac{1}{4}$ cup) cocoa
6 oz. dates
little egg

*Or plain flour with $1\frac{1}{2}$ level teaspoons baking powder

Cream the butter and sugar until soft in texture. Sieve the flour and cocoa or flour, baking powder and cocoa and work into the butter mixture. Chop the dates finely then knead into the mixture and gradually add just enough egg to make a slightly sticky texture. Grease and flour two flat baking trays and put teaspoons of the mixture on to these, allowing room for them to spread out. Bake in the centre of a very moderate oven, 325–350°F, Mark 3–4, for approximately 20 minutes until very firm. Cool on the trays, then store in an air-tight tin.
Makes about 24–30.

Variations:
Add about 2 oz. ($\frac{1}{2}$ cup) chopped nuts.
Add $\frac{1}{2}$ teaspoon ground cinnamon.
Use half sugar and half honey to sweeten the cookies.

Chocolate date fingers: Use the recipe above, and knead very well when adding the dates. Try to omit the egg altogether or use a very small amount to give a soft rolling consistency. Roll out to about $\frac{1}{3}$-inch in thickness, cut into fingers, bake as above for about 15 minutes. Cool and store. Top with a little icing (made as page 99).

118

Breadcrumb Cookies

4 oz. ($\frac{1}{2}$ cup) butter or white fat
4 oz. ($\frac{1}{2}$ cup) sugar*
1 level tablespoon golden syrup
4 oz. (1 cup) fine crisp
  breadcrumbs

4 oz. (1 cup) self-raising flour**
$\frac{1}{2}$ level teaspoon baking powder**
pinch ground ginger
very little milk (optional)

*Either all white or half white and half brown sugar.
**Or plain flour and 1$\frac{1}{2}$ level teaspoons baking powder

Cream the butter or fat and sugar with the syrup until soft.
Add the breadcrumbs and the flour sieved with the baking
powder and ginger. Knead very firmly to bind together. Add
only as much milk as necessary, you may find you need no
milk. Roll into small balls, if the mixture becomes slightly
crumbly, then damp your fingers. Grease 2 baking trays and
put the balls on to this, allowing space for the biscuits to
spread out. Bake for 15 minutes in the centre of a very
moderate oven, 325–350°F, Mark 3–4. Cool on the baking
trays.
Makes about 20.

Coconut Shortbreads

3 oz. ($\frac{3}{8}$ cup) butter
2 oz. ($\frac{1}{4}$ cup) sugar
3 oz. ($\frac{3}{4}$ cup) self-raising flour*

1 oz. ($\frac{1}{3}$ cup) desiccated coconut
decoration:
desiccated coconut
glacé cherries

*Or plain flour sieved with $\frac{3}{4}$ teaspoon baking powder

Cream the butter and sugar, work in the flour or flour and
baking powder and coconut. Form into small balls and roll in
coconut. Put on to lightly greased baking trays, allowing
room for them to spread. Top each biscuit with a small piece
of glacé cherry and bake as the cookies above.
Makes about 15.

Strawberry Shortcake

8 oz. (2 cups) self-raising flour*
2 oz. ($\frac{1}{4}$ cup) margarine or butter
2 oz. ($\frac{1}{4}$ cup) sugar
milk to mix

Filling:
little sugar
strawberries
thick cream

*Or plain flour with 2 teaspoons baking powder

Sieve the flour into a mixing bowl, rub in the margarine or butter. Add the sugar and mix to a fairly firm rolling consistency with the milk. Knead the dough lightly to give a smooth mixture. Divide into 2 equal portions and form into two 8–9-inch rounds, or put into lightly greased 8–9-inch shallow sandwich or cake tins. Bake just above the centre of a hot oven, 425–450°F, Mark 6–7, for about 15 minutes or until firm and golden brown. Turn out, allow to cool then sandwich together with sweetened fruit and whipped cream. Top with fruit and cream.
Serves 4–6.
This is the most economical type of shortcake that can be varied in very many ways.

Shortbread Biscuits

4 oz. ($\frac{1}{2}$ cup) butter
3 oz. (scant cup) sieved icing sugar

6 oz. ($1\frac{1}{2}$ cups) plain flour
flavouring, see method

Cream the butter and sugar until soft. Add the flour and flavouring, and knead well until smooth. Roll out to about $\frac{1}{4}$ inch in thickness. Cut into fingers or rounds. Put on to an ungreased baking tray and prick with a fork, this prevents the mixture rising, and bake in the centre of a very moderate oven, 325°F, Mark 3. Cool on the baking tray.
Flavourings:
Add the grated rind, but not juice, of a lemon.
Add a good pinch mixed spice or other spice.
Variation:
Shortbread Round: Use recipe above or increase butter by 1 oz. Press into an 8-inch tin. Prick, and bake for 30 minutes in slow to very moderate oven, 300–325°F, Mark 2–3.

Supper Snacks

These snacks are simple enough for the younger members of the family to prepare.

Surprise Sausages

1 lb. sausages
2 oz. Cheddar cheese
8 rashers long streaky bacon
Sauce:
2 oz. (1 cup) soft breadcrumbs

1 onion
$\frac{1}{2}$ pint ($1\frac{1}{3}$ cups) milk
1 oz. butter or margarine
seasoning

Grill or fry the sausages until nearly cooked. This can be done earlier in the day. Split and insert pieces of cheese. Take the rinds from the bacon and twist round the sausages; secure with wooden cocktail sticks if necessary. Put in a dish and place near the top of a moderately hot oven, 375–400°F, Mark 5–6, and cook for about 12 minutes. These can be served with tomato ketchup or mustard, but the bread sauce recipe, normally served with chicken, is particularly good here.

Bread Sauce:

Put the breadcrumbs, whole peeled onion, milk, butter or margarine and a little seasoning into a saucepan. Bring the mixture to the boil, stir well, then leave in a warm place for as long as possible – at least 30 minutes. Reheat, stirring well so the mixture does not burn. Remove the onion and serve. The sauce can be cooked in a covered container in the coolest part of the oven. Cover well, so it does not dry on top, and use a large sized container, so the mixture does not boil over.

Variations:

Use frankfurter sausages instead of cooked sausages. Spread the split sausages with chutney or mustard instead of cheese. Make a more complete meal by baking halved seasoned tomatoes in the dish with the sausages, etc.

SANDWICHES

Sandwiches are one of the easiest of supper snacks and the following recipes are substantial enough to make a satisfying meal. Serve with some kind of salad (if not included in the sandwich) and with fresh fruit, so that the meal is a well balanced one.

Filled Sandwiches

Spread brown and white or rye or other breads with butter or margarine. The sandwiches look more original if you use one white slice and one brown or rye bread slice.

Some meat fillings:
Blend chopped hard boiled eggs with diced liver sausage and a little mayonnaise.
Mix diced chicken, diced cooked ham and mayonnaise.
Crumble crisply fried bacon and mix with chopped hard boiled eggs and chopped watercress.

Some fish fillings:
Blend flaked canned salmon or tuna with chopped gherkins (or cucumber), a little chopped parsley and mayonnaise.
Mix mashed sardines with chopped spring onions or scallions and chopped hard boiled eggs – flavour with a few drops of lemon juice.
Blend grated cheese, chopped anchovy fillets and mayonnaise together.

Open Sandwiches

Top the buttered bread with lettuce and then the foods; here are some easy suggestions:

Hawaiian sandwiches:
Top with sliced or cream cheese, twists of fresh or canned pineapple and crisp bacon.

122

Seafood sandwiches:
Top with flaked canned or cooked salmon, prawns and anchovy fillets. Top with thick mayonnaise and twists of lemon and cucumber.

Chicken supper snack:
Top slices of chicken with mayonnaise, garnish with crisp bacon and Russian salad.

DRINKS

One of the dangers of modern living is that we all eat too much between meals – sweetmeats, ice cream, potato crisps, etc. This leads to over-weight in adults and in children and also tends to spoil one's appetite for the more nourishing main protein dishes; it also aids tooth decay. Try to avoid this habit as much as possible and do not encourage children to have starchy foods between their main meals.

Drinks:
Choose fresh fruit juices rather than sweetened squashes, etc. or have tea and coffee with little if any sugar.

Foods:
Eat fresh fruit, raw carrots, celery, dried fruits (raisins, etc.) instead of sweets and buns. When children are very hungry offer diced cheese, nuts and apples or celery, not sticky buns or sweets.

Following page: FRUIT MILK SHAKE

MILK SHAKES

This is an excellent way of encouraging all the family to enjoy milk

To give a fruit flavour:
Use fruit flavoured syrups, made especially to use in milk
shakes; also blackcurrant and rose hip syrups or crushed
fresh fruit.
If you have a liquidizer the methods of making the drinks are
very simple; there are several ways to achieve these fluffy
mixtures. Remember the liquidizer aerates the milk, so to
produce a full tumbler of milk shake use barely $\frac{3}{4}$ tumbler of
milk.
Put 1–2 tablespoons syrup and the hot or cold milk into the
goblet. Put the lid on firmly and switch to the highest speed.
Maintain for about 30 seconds to 1 minute. Pour into the
tumbler.
Put a little crushed ice in the goblet with the syrup and milk.
Switch on as described above. Put a spoonful of ice cream into
the goblet, then add the syrup and milk. Switch on as
described above.
Put fresh fruit, a few strawberries, piece of apple, orange or
banana, into the goblet. Add the hot or cold milk. You can
use crushed ice, or ice cream with cold milk. Switch on as
described above.
If you have no liquidizer – use the suggestions below. The
mixture does not become quite as aerated, so use a little more
milk to fill the tumbler:
Put into a cocktail shaker and shake hard.
Put into a jug or basin and whisk vigorously.

Chocolate and Coffee Milk Shakes

Use one of the methods of mixing given above, but flavour
the milk with a little cocoa or chocolate powder, instant
coffee, coffee essence, or strong coffee.

Preceding page: COFFEE MILK SHAKE

Index